THE SOUL OF GRAMMAR

T0382292

THE SOUL OF GRAMMAR

A Bird's-eye View of the Organic Unity of the
Ancient & the Modern Languages studied
in British and American Schools

By

E. A. SONNENSCHEIN

D.Litt. Oxon.

*Emeritus Professor of Classics in the University
of Birmingham; Chairman of the Standing
Committee on Grammatical Reform; some-
time Chairman of the Joint Committee
on the Terminology of Grammar and
of the Oriental Advisory Committee on the Terminology and
Classifications of Grammar*

EVOLUTION, NOT REVOLUTION

CAMBRIDGE
AT THE UNIVERSITY PRESS
MCMXXVII

CAMBRIDGE
UNIVERSITY PRESS

University Printing House, Cambridge CB2 8BS, United Kingdom

Published in the United States of America by Cambridge University Press, New York

Cambridge University Press is part of the University of Cambridge.

It furthers the University's mission by disseminating knowledge in the pursuit of
education, learning and research at the highest international levels of excellence.

www.cambridge.org
Information on this title: www.cambridge.org/9781107654907

© Cambridge University Press 1922

First published 1922
First paperback edition 2014

A catalogue record for this publication is available from the British Library

ISBN 978-1-107-65490-7 Paperback

PREFACE

"The hand of the Lord was upon me,...and set me down in the midst of the valley which was full of bones,...and, behold, there were very many in the open valley; and, lo, they were very dry....So I prophesied as I was commanded: and as I prophesied, there was a noise, and behold a shaking, and the bones came together, bone to his bone...and the breath came into them, and they lived." (Ezekiel xxxvii. 1–10.)

GRAMMAR is usually considered a dry subject, and attempts have been made, especially in recent times, to render it more interesting. Can these dry bones live? And how are they to be quickened? The above quotation from the Hebrew prophet suggests an answer. The breath of life can be breathed into them if they are treated not bone by bone but as members of a great organism wherein thought and feeling find expression. To the advanced student grammar is a fascinating subject, just because he knows that he is dealing with an organic unity— a unity analogous to that with which the astronomer feels himself in contact when he studies the movements and the constitution of the heavenly bodies. To the scientific grammarian language is a little universe—a microcosm governed by law and order and therefore intelligible, not a chaos.

Language is a product of the human mind, and reflects its operations. In so far, then, as the human mind is one and the same all the world over, human speech is bound to exhibit some common features wherever it comes into being. Hence the idea of a Universal Grammar: "Grammatica nihil aliud est quam quaedam inalterabilis locutionis identitas diversis temporibus atque locis" wrote Dante in his De Vulgari Eloquentia (I. ix). And Bacon conceived of a "nobilissima grammaticae species" which should compare the features of many tongues "both learned and vulgar" and by combining their several distinctive excellences arrive at something like an ideal medium of expression (De Dignitate et Augmentis Scientiarum, Book VI. i).

Such conceptions of the nature and purpose of grammar were wide-spread in the 18th century; but the science of comparative grammar, as understood at the present day, sets itself a more modest task. It finds enough to do in examining and classifying the usages of particular languages, ancient and modern, and so arriving at an understanding of their historical development and their relations to one another. Thus the idea of a universal grammar, based on universal laws of human thought, has receded into the background. It is generally and rightly felt that any such system of grammar would have to be something very abstract, and that it might be found to involve the same difficulties as that "metaphysical grammar" which the world of to-day has left behind it. For languages are not all cut out on the same pattern: the mind of man has not worked in exactly the same way at all times and in all races.

On the other hand, comparative grammar has definitely established the existence of certain families of human speech, which it classifies according to their affinities of structure. Each family is recognized as forming a unity, and as differing in structure from other families. Thus it is still possible to speak of a "common grammar" in the sense of a grammatical system which is applicable not indeed to all languages but to all the languages of one family. And, as a matter of fact, the main effort of comparative grammarians is directed to drawing the outlines of common grammars, and so enabling the student to trace a community of structure in a whole group of languages. As a conspicuous example may be mentioned the great work on the comparative grammar of the Indo-European family by Brugmann and Delbrück, and the masterly compendium of results written by the former scholar—entitled Kurze Vergleichende Grammatik der Indogermanischen Sprachen (Strassburg, 1904)—to which the present treatise is largely indebted.

The community of structure of the Eastern and the Western branches of the Indo-European family is attested by a curious fact, to which perhaps too little attention has been paid. So early as the fifth century B.C., i.e. long before the conquests of Alexander the Great had brought the West into contact with the East, the ancient Hindu grammarians had constructed a system of grammar for Sanskrit which was fundamentally the same as that which was devised at a somewhat later date, but without any knowledge of Sanskrit grammar, by the Greek grammarians for Greek. In both these independent systems Cases, Voices, Moods, Tenses, Numbers, and Persons were classified on the same principles. How could this have come about, had it not been that the Sanskrit and the Greek languages were fundamentally one in structure? When the same key is found to open two locks, we are justified in inferring that the locks are similarly constructed.

The object of the present essay is to bring home to the minds of my readers the fact that the languages of prime importance to our Western civilization—whether ancient or modern—are fundamentally one in structure. Such an attempt is not uncalled for at the present day. For though the general results of comparative grammar are undisputed, few people are aware of the extent to which the modern languages of our family are syntactically akin to the ancient tongues of Greece and of Rome. And, what is more, some writers whose position in the world of scholarship commands respect are inclined to dispute the fact. The champions of this negative attitude do not, as a rule, deny that languages like English and French belong to the Indo-European family; but they nevertheless declare that there is little or no real resemblance between the structure of modern languages and that of ancient languages! Professor Jespersen of Copenhagen goes even further, by insisting on a process of "differentiation which in course of time has torn asunder languages that were at first closely akin"[1]. I do not believe in this breach of continuity; and in this essay I set forth the grounds of the faith that is in me by showing that the categories of Case, Mood, and Tense, devised by the Greek and the Hindu grammarians, are applicable without violence to modern languages— *provided that these categories are properly understood and defined.* This proviso is all-important. But, subject to it, I hold that the old grammatical categories are realities at the present day—in other words, that the grammarian of a modern language is justified in thinking in terms of these categories, indeed that he is bound to do so, if he aims at a really scientific understanding of the usages of modern languages. At any rate it is

---

[1] The Philosophy of Grammar (1924), p. 178.

my hope that my readers will find that new light is thrown
upon many a modern construction by regarding it from a comparative and historical point of view.

My argument involves no "forcing of modern languages into
the framework of ancient languages", no "invention of resem-
blances which do not in fact exist". It simply discloses an
actually existing identity of structure, which is disguised, but
not annihilated, by external changes of form. The outer forms
of the Cases, Moods, and Tenses have suffered great changes in
the course of time, but their inner meanings or functions are
in the main what they were in the earliest days of which we
have any cognizance. That there are some real differences between languages of the same family is, of course, indisputable;
and in the present essay I not only admit the fact but am careful
to call attention to the divergences as well as the agreements
in the several languages here studied. The nature and the extent
of the former, however, are best studied in the light of the
latter—as instances of diversity within a unity. The general
conclusion which I aim at establishing is summed up at the
end of my first chapter (§ 70) and in the Retrospect at the end
of the volume.

For the effective comparison of different languages uniformity
of grammatical nomenclature is absolutely essential. I have here
availed myself of the grammatical terms recommended by the
British and American Committees that have drawn up reports
on the matter[1].

The reader of this book is assumed to have a working knowledge of some at least of the six languages here treated in outline.

[1] On the Terminology of Grammar, being the Report of the Joint-Committee on Grammatical Terminology (London, John Murray; revised
1911 and subsequently reprinted; seventh impression 1922).—Report of
the Joint-Committee on Grammatical Nomenclature (Washington, D. C.;
first edition 1913; revised edition 1923).—Report of the Oriental Advisory
Committee on the Terminology and Classifications of Grammar (Oxford,
Clarendon Press, 1920; dealing with Indo-Aryan languages, ancient and
modern).

Any differences between the recommendations of the British and the
American Joint-Committees are mentioned in foot-notes.

My hope is that my sketch may be found useful by teachers and by students in universities and training colleges, and perhaps also in the highest forms of schools, as enabling them to take a bird's-eye view of the outstanding relations of the languages in which they are interested, and to survey as a whole the field which they have already cultivated in parts. My object, however, has not been to exhaust the subject, but rather to concentrate attention on its most important aspects—the syntax of nouns and verbs—and to leave matters of secondary importance to incidental treatment. Thus in my first chapter I touch incidentally upon the functions of Order of Words and Intonation (§§ 11, 77) and also upon the constructions used with the Passive Voice (§§ 24–26, 35, 37); and in my treatment of Moods and Tenses I take the structure of Sentences and Clauses in my stride. In this way I hope I have covered the ground sufficiently for the purpose in hand.

My best thanks are due to several friends who have aided me in my work. Professor Kroll of Breslau and my former pupil Professor Mountford of Cornell University have been so good as to read the book in type-script, and have made many helpful suggestions. Another former pupil of mine, Dr Henry Thomas of the British Museum, has kindly revised and added to my Spanish examples. I am also indebted for sympathetic criticism to the Standing Committee on Grammatical Reform, whose members however are not responsible, individually or collectively, for any views expressed in this volume.

In the Addenda (p. 116) I have briefly indicated my obligations to other friends who have aided me by their counsel in the course of my work or by comments on my proof sheets— Professor Macdonell and Mr Onions of Oxford, Professor Pearson of Cambridge, Dr Mackail of London, and others.

I desire also to acknowledge with thanks the care bestowed upon the proof sheets by the readers of the University Press.

E. A. S.

4 SION HILL PLACE
    BATH

CONTENTS

CHAPTER I

ON CASES AND CASE-PHRASES

§ 1. What is a Case? The Latin word *casus*, from which the English 'case' is derived, was a translation of the Greek πτῶσις, the literal meaning of which was 'fall' or 'deflection'. It was this literal sense which suggested to some Greek grammarian the idea of representing the relation of the nominative to the accusative, the genitive, and the dative by means of a diagram. The nominative was depicted by an upright line, and the other three cases by lines lying obliquely to it: hence the name πτώσεις πλάγιαι 'oblique cases'. But according to this diagram the nominative was excluded from the list of cases; for it was not a 'deflection'. And the grammarians of the Peripatetic school did not call it a case. But at a later date the Stoic grammarians declared the nominative to be a case, and called it the πτῶσις ὀρθή 'upright case'. This seems to show that they were no longer dominated by the literal sense of the term πτῶσις; otherwise πτῶσις ὀρθή 'upright deflection' would have involved an absurd contradiction in terms. The Stoics must, in fact, have understood the term πτῶσις in a wider sense, as denoting not 'deflection' but '*situation* in relation to other words in the sentence'.[1] From this point of view the figurative expression πτῶσις ὀρθή 'upright situation' presented no difficulty. It is this wider sense of the term which we still have in mind when we speak of 'cases' in grammar. The English word 'case' is also thus used in such expressions as 'You and I are in the same case' (i.e. in the same situation or predicament or plight); 'My case is different from yours'. The history of the German noun *Fall* presents an interesting parallel to that of the Greek πτῶσις. Originally it denoted 'fall' in the literal sense (e.g. the fall of a tree). The fall of dice suggested expressions like *ein glücklicher Fall* 'a lucky throw'; and the term acquired the meaning of

[1] Still wider senses of the term are found in Aristotle.

'situation' (= *Lage*) in expressions like *ein harter Fall* 'a hard case', *in diesem Falle* 'in this case'. And, like πτῶσις and *casus*, the German *Fall* came to be used in grammar in the technical sense of 'case.'

§ 2. What were the distinguishing features of these 'cases'? They differed from one another in two respects: they always differed in meaning, and they generally (though not always) differed in form. The first difference may be called 'functional' and the second 'morphological'. Now it is evident that the ancient grammarians took account of both these features. Their terms denoting the several cases were *functional terms applied to the forms of words*; that is to say, they classified and named the forms according to their meanings and uses in sentences. The forms were not necessarily all different from one another; for the same form might be used with more than one meaning: e.g. the forms γένος, ὄνομα, πειθώ served as nominative, vocative, and accusative singular, and the form πόλεις as nominative, vocative, and accusative plural. Nor were the forms necessarily inflected; for the uninflected stem of a word might serve as a case (e.g. ὤρα- as nom. sing.; μέλαν-, εὐγενέσ-, etc., as nom. or acc. sing. neut.). It is very necessary to arrive at a clear understanding on this point; for it is commonly misunderstood. It is generally supposed that the 'declension' of a word is a purely morphological classification. But a little reflection shows that this is not so.

§ 3. The declension of a word is a classification of its forms according to their meanings and uses in sentences[1]. Thus in Latin the declension of the word meaning 'thing'—a typical noun of the fifth declension—is exhibited in the following shape:

Nom.	Sing.	*res*	Nom.	Plur.	*res*
Voc.	Sing.	*res*	Voc.	Plur.	*res*
Acc.	Sing.	*rem*	Acc.	Plur.	*res*
Gen.	Sing.	*rei*	Gen.	Plur.	*rerum*
Dat.	Sing.	*rei*	Dat.	Plur.	*rebus*
Abl.	Sing.	*re*	Abl.	Plur.	*rebus*

[1] "The grouping and the naming of the cases proceed according to their meaning, not according to their form; so that not only are different forms

Here we have only six forms (*res, rem, rei, re, rerum, rebus*), but twice that number of cases (six singular and six plural), the meanings of which are roughly indicated by their names. And in the other declensions the number of cases is always in excess of the number of forms. So too in Greek: for example, the nominative δῶρον and the accusative δῶρον are two different cases of the word meaning 'gift'.

§ 4. It is evident, then, that the term πτῶσις did not necessarily involve a difference of form[1]: two cases might differ functionally without differing morphologically. Thus the ancient grammarians must have conceived of a case as a form having, or capable of having, a particular meaning in a sentence, without necessarily showing that meaning outwardly. For the same form often had different meanings in different sentences, and therefore did not *in itself* express any meaning distinctly. Such forms were, in fact, ambiguous: e.g. δῶρον or *res*. The meaning of such a form in any particular sentence was shown sometimes by the order of words, sometimes by the phrasing and intonation of the sentence, sometimes by the context in which the form stood, or very often by a combination of two or three different agencies working together. It constantly happens that the case of a Greek or Latin word cannot be determined until the reader has examined the rest of the sentence. The form *Romae* is in some contexts a genitive, in others a dative, in others a locative (compare Horace, Odes iv. 3. 13 with Satires ii. 1. 59); *Athenis* may be either a dative (*Athenis dedit* 'he gave to Athens') or an ablative denoting 'from' (*Athenis discessit* 'he departed from Athens'), or a locatival ablative denoting 'at' (*Athenis vivebat*); *Praeneste* may be either a nominative or an accusative or an ablative (Horace, Epist. i. 2. 2) according to its context; *deum* and *divum* may be either accusative singular or genitive plural; and so forth.

sometimes classified under a common name (e.g. ἵπποιο and θεᾶς under the name 'genitive singular'), but also identical or related forms are separated from one another (e.g. the nom. sing. fem. and the nom. and acc. plural neuter)." Karl Brugmann, Kurze Vergleichende Grammatik, § 452 (2), p. 373 (abbreviated).

[1] This is explicitly stated by that great authority on the Greek πτώσεις, the late Professor Bywater, in his note on Aristotle's Poetics, ch. xx (1457 a).

In Catullus 9. 5 *o mihi nuntii beati!* the word *nuntii* is taken by
most commentators as a vocative plural (denoting 'pieces of
news'); but by some, including Professor Kroll (1923), as a
genitive singular (gen. of exclamation). Everything here depends
on how the context is interpreted. Was the poet thinking of
several separate pieces of news or of only one?[1] The rôle of
order of words and of phrasing and intonation will be illustrated
below in connexion with modern languages (§ 11).

It may be added that the exact meaning of a case (i.e. the
precise meaning which the speaker or writer intended the form
to have) was *never* shown by the case-form alone; for every one
of the cases had a certain *range* of meaning, as will be illustrated
below (§ 7), and the case-form never indicated more than this
general range of meaning, under which the particular instance
fell. The case-form *contributed* in varying degrees to the indication of the meaning; but the value of its contribution depended
on how far the form was distinctive. Thus the form *rerum* contributed more to the indication of a particular meaning than did
the form *rei* (genitive or dative), and still more than the form
res, which belonged to four different cases (singular or plural).

§ 5. The names denoting the cases are, it is true, not happy
terms: they are derived from Latin translations of Greek terms
which were themselves not very successful attempts at describing
the functions of the cases. But they were *intended* to be descriptive of these functions—the 'naming' case (ὀνομαστική, *nomi-
nativus*), the 'calling' or 'addressing' case (κλητική or προσ-
αγορευτική, *vocativus*), the 'causal' case (αἰτιατική or αἰτιολο-
γική, *accusativus*), the 'generic' or 'possessive' case (γενική or
κτητική, *genetivus* or *possessivus*), the case of 'giving' or 'com-
mending' (δοτική or ἐπισταλτική, *dativus* or *commendativus*),
the 'taking away' case (*ablativus*, not in Greek)[2]. Such terms

---

[1] A choice of cases arises in many passages of Virgil, e.g. Aen. ii. 223
(*mugitus*), 246 (*fatis*), 247 (*credita*), 250 (*oceano*).

[2] The term *ablativus* was the creation of some Roman grammarian of
the first century B.C., prior to Julius Caesar, who used the term in his
De Analogia. Varro called the case *casus sextus* or *casus Latinus* (as being
peculiar to Latin). The name of the corresponding Sanskrit case was
apādāna (from *apa*=ἀπό, a preposition, *dāna* 'taking').

have nothing to do with morphology. When we want to describe not the functions but the forms of cases, we use quite different terms; we say, for example, that *rebus* is a vowel-stem with the suffix *-bus*, and *res* the same stem with the suffix *-s*. And if the declension of *res* were arranged on this morphological principle, it would present an entirely different face from that which it actually has.

§6. It may be worth while to dwell for a moment on two of these curious case-names—the 'accusative' and the 'genitive'. The noun αἰτία, from which the adjective αἰτιατικός is derived, had two meanings: (i) *responsibility, guilt*, or the imputation thereof, i.e. *accusation*; (ii) *cause*, i.e. that which produces a certain effect. It was the second of these meanings that the Greek grammarians had in mind when they devised the grammatical term αἰτιατικὴ πτῶσις 'causal case'. But to the Romans this term suggested the idea of accusation, and they therefore mistranslated it as *casus accusativus*. There is, however, some difficulty in discovering exactly what the Greeks meant by calling the case 'causal'. In some instances it clearly denotes *that which is caused or effected*, e.g. ὕλη φύει φύλλα 'a forest puts forth leaves', οἰκοδομῶ τεῖχος 'I am building a wall'. But in what sense is the accusative 'causal' in the commoner instances in which it denotes that which is *affected* by an action, e.g. φιλῶ τὸν Σωκράτην 'I love Socrates', οἱ Ἀθηναῖοι ἀπέκτειναν τὸν Σωκράτην 'the Athenians put Socrates to death'? Did the grammarians regard this use of the case as analogous to the other? Or did they think of the object as, in a sense, *causative*, i.e. *causing* the action in such instances? Modern psychologists speak of the object as a 'stimulus' to the action of the subject. When a dog gnaws a bone, his action is stimulated by the bone. I am tempted to quote the following French limerick:

> Il était un homme de Madère
> Qui cassa la tête à son père.
> On demanda "Pourquoi?"
> Il répondit "Ma foi!
> Vous n'avez pas connu mon père."

It is worth noticing that Priscian (ii. 185) uses the term *causativus*, side by side with *accusativus*, as a name of this case.

The term γενική 'genitive' (from γένος 'kind', 'class') signified *classifying* and *defining*: e.g. ὁ πρῶτος τῶν πολιτῶν 'the first of the citizens', ἡ οἰκία τοῦ Περικλέους 'the house of Pericles' (the Periclean house). This meaning is not expressed by the Latin term *genetivus* (so correctly spelled), which is more like another Greek name for the case—πατρική: for *genetivus* means literally 'connected with birth or origin'. The Romans, too, sometimes called the case *patricus* or *paternus*.

§ 7. To find appropriate names for the cases was no easy task; for all the cases admitted of being used in more than one way, i.e. with functions that were more or less distinct (see § 4, end); nor were the functions of one case always logically distinct from those of another. This is by no means surprising when we remember that languages are not the creations of logical or philosophical reflexion, and are therefore often defective as instruments of expression and communication. Yet though it is impossible to draw a clear logical distinction between certain uses of different cases[1], there are broad distinctions of meaning between all the cases—distinctions which come out with perfect clearness in the most important of their uses, and which were therefore taken as typical and employed as a basis for classifying and naming the cases in ancient times. The modern grammarian is confronted with the same difficulty as was felt by the old Greek grammarians, and he must solve it on the same principle as they did. Names more aptly descriptive of the functions of the cases may conceivably be found some day. But it is only by their imperfectly demarcated spheres of meaning that the cases can ever be defined or named; for there are no generally

---

[1] For example, the dative sometimes approaches very near to the accusative in meaning: compare *it clamor caelo* 'a shout rises to the sky' (Virgil, Aen. v. 451) and ἀνατείνας οὐρανῷ χεῖρας (Pindar, Isthm. 5. 41) with *it domum* 'he is going home' and κνίση οὐρανὸν ἷκε (Iliad i. 317). Again the dative is logically equivalent to a genitive in instances like *Philocomasio amator* 'the lover of Philocomasium' (Plautus, Mil. 1431, cf. 271). In *civibus libertatem ademit* 'he took liberty away from his fellow-citizens' the dative is logically equivalent to an ablative. Yet all these meanings of the dative belong to one psychologically associated group of meanings.

available morphological differentiae on which definitions or names of the cases can be based.

§ 8. Nor is it an easy matter to define the term 'case' itself. Many modern writers have defined it in too narrow a sense, so as to limit it to *distinctive* forms, i.e. forms which *show* a case-relation. This definition is sometimes given or at any rate implied by writers of Latin grammars, though it is never applied in practice. If it were, not a single Latin noun or pronoun or adjective could be said to have its full complement of cases: for example, nouns of the 1st declension and nouns in *us* of the 2nd and 4th declensions could not be said to have either a genitive singular or a nominative plural; for the forms *mensae, domini,* and *gradūs* are not distinctive of either of these cases. Nor could any Latin word be said to have an ablative plural as distinct from a dative plural. This definition, then, cannot be right. Yet it is employed with great confidence by some writers on English grammar, as though it were an obvious fact that no form can be called a case, unless it distinctly *shows* a case-relation. The result has been wide-spread uncertainty as to how many cases there are in English[1]. Some writers recognize only one case of English nouns (the genitive or possessive), on the ground that English nouns have only one form that shows a case-relation by an inflexion; others, regarding both the inflected form (e.g. *man's*) and the uninflected form (e.g. *man*) as distinctive—the one of the genitival relation, the other of relations other than that of the genitive—recognize two cases, and call the second of them the 'common case'. But this term will not bear examination. The *form* of this so-called case is no doubt common, i.e. common to several distinct case-relations; but in what sense can the *case* be called common? Common to what? The incongruity of the term 'common' is clearly seen by comparing it with the term 'genitive' or 'possessive', which these grammarians use side by side with it. 'Genitive' and 'possessive' are functional terms descriptive

[1] English grammar has gradually advanced from the denial of the existence of any cases of nouns to the recognition of four or five cases, as I have shown in The School World, 1913, p. 256, in Modern Language Teaching, 1915 (Vol. XI), and in the Preface to Part II of my New English Grammar (Oxford, 1916).

of a relation; but 'common' is descriptive not of a relation but only of a form. Moreover the term 'common case' (or any less objectionable substitute for it that might be found) serves no useful purpose in grammar; for it confuses under a common name three relations which are distinct and which must be somehow distinguished from one another in terminology—the relations of the subject, the direct object, and the indirect object (e.g. in the sentence '*John* gave the *man money*')[1]. A third school of grammarians, dating from the time of Lindley Murray (i.e. the beginning of the nineteenth century), recognize three cases of English nouns, which they call nominative, genitive, and objective. This classification is on the right lines, and it has been widely adopted. But the functional term 'objective' is open to two objections: (*a*) it confuses under a common name two distinct relations—that of the direct object and that of the indirect object; (*b*) it is a misnomer when applied to the case-relation of the nouns in 'Go *home*', 'I have been living here twenty *years*', etc.; for this relation is not that of an object in any ordinary sense of the term.

§ 9. I offer the following definition of the difficult term 'case', as expressing what the Stoics meant by a πτῶσις (cf. § 4) and as applicable to all languages that have cases; and I will adhere to it throughout this book: *A case is a form of a noun or pronoun or adjective standing, or capable of standing, in one of a particular group of relations to some other member or members of a sentence.* That relation is not necessarily shown by the form itself, i.e. the form need not be *distinctive*. of the relation; but the form may serve as one

---

[1] Professor Jespersen of Copenhagen advocates the two-case doctrine with a fervour all his own (Philosophy of Grammar, 1924, pp. 173–184; cf. p. 119 and p. 141, where the offending term 'common case' is used without any attempt to explain or justify it). This doctrine he supports by the alleged impossibility of finding any truly grammatical criterion, *whether of form or of function*, whereby a dative can be distinguished from an accusative in modern English (p. 174). Here I part company with Jespersen. As to the nominative he says nothing explicitly, but he apparently holds that there is no criterion whereby a nominative can now be distinguished from an accusative or a dative of an English noun. He is evidently dominated by a narrow conception of the meaning of the term 'case'. Compare § 15, note, p. 19.

of the agencies whereby the relation is indicated. Highly inflected languages have, of course, a larger proportion of distinctive forms than less highly inflected languages[1].

§ 10. This definition bears a certain resemblance to that which is given by writers of the school of Wundt, but it differs from their definition in one essential point. Wundt made no attempt to interpret the term 'case' in its traditional sense: he gave an entirely new meaning to the term by treating it as denoting *any expression of a case-relation*. Professor Max Deutschbein, a disciple of Wundt, defines the term as follows: "Case is the linguistic expression of the relation in which an idea signified by a noun or a pronoun stands to the other members of the sentence" (translated from his System der neuenglischen Syntax, 1917, p. 256). This definition includes, and is intended to include, among cases every combination of a preposition with a case—not only combinations that are *equivalent* to cases, such as *of John* (= John's), *to me* (= me; e.g. 'Give the book to me' = 'Give me the book'), but also combinations like *in London, from London, before dawn, after sunset, among us, with him, without her, by them, because of them*, and so forth. According to this definition there are in every language, in addition to the cases that consist of a single word, at least as many 'cases' as there are prepositions—nay more; for many of the prepositions are capable of indicating more than one relation. But this involves a revolution in the meaning of the term 'case'; for the preposition (πρόθεσις, *praepositio*) has always been treated by grammarians as a separate part of speech, and from this point of view the combination of a preposition with a case cannot be identified with a case standing alone[2].

§ 11. But my definition of 'case', like Wundt's, does not demand distinctive forms of nouns, pronouns, or adjectives as a *sine qua non* of distinct cases; for form is only one of several agencies whereby

---

[1] In the above definition it is of course assumed that the relations in which words stand to one another in a sentence correspond to the relations of the things or activities denoted by the words.

[2] The treatment of 'case' in Grattan and Gurrey's Our Living Language (1925) is based on this innovation in the definition of the term 'case'.

distinctions of case may be indicated. The part played by agencies other than form in indicating case-relations is especially important in languages that have few distinctive forms.

(i) *Order of words.* All languages have certain habits of arranging the words of sentences in a certain sequence, and from these usages they do not depart except for good reason. The effect of these usages is that the habitual order of words, when once established, serves as an auxiliary agency in indicating the relations in which the component elements in a sentence stand to one another. But in no language is the order of words immutably fixed, just as on the other hand there is no language in which it is absolutely free. The habitual order of words is not a hard and fast rule; for it is always liable to be crossed by the desire of the speaker or writer to give prominence to a particular word, and also by considerations of euphony and rhythm. But in the absence of any such disturbing influences the speaker or writer follows the habitual order; and the hearer or reader accepts the habitual order as a clue to the meaning, unless he has some reason to think that the order of words has been inverted.

The subject, if expressed by a separate word, habitually precedes the predicate in most Indo-European languages[1]; and in most of the modern languages of our family this order of words is the chief clue to the meaning of the sentence, enabling the hearer or reader to distinguish the subject from the object; for the object is a part of the predicate. Thus there is no ambiguity in sentences like the following, though the object-case has the same *form* as the subject-case: 'the lion beat the unicorn', 'das Mädchen liebt das Kätzlein', 'Brutus tua César'. But in Spanish the object may often be distinguished from the subject by the preposition *a*: e.g. 'Bruto mató a César'. In English and German the contribution of the *forms* of the nouns to the expression of the meaning is very small; but at any rate these forms (*lion, unicorn, Mädchen, Kätzlein*) differ from genitives (*lion's, unicorn's, Mädchens, Kätzleins*) and are therefore indicative to some small extent of the meaning of the speaker or writer. In more highly inflected languages the order of words is far less important, because the

---

[1] Celtic languages are an exception, e.g. Welsh.

subject-case usually (not always) differs in form from the object-case: but even in Greek and Latin the habitual order of subject before predicate creates a presumption that of two words, denoting respectively the subject and the object, the one that stands first is the subject, even if it does not differ in form from an accusative; thus in sentences like the following, in which both the subject and the object stand in the accusative case, the order of words is the main clue to the meaning: Συνέβη τῆς αὐτῆς ἡμέρης ἔν τε τῇ Σικελίῃ Γέλωνα καὶ Θήρωνα νικᾶν Ἀμίλκαν τὸν Καρχηδόνιον καὶ ἐν Σαλαμῖνι τοὺς Ἕλληνας τὸν Πέρσην (Herodotus vii. 166); *Is mihi dixit se Athenis me exspectaturum* (Cicero, ad Att. vi. 3. 9; cf. iii. 14. 1). The face value of the oracular response *Aio te, Aeacida, Romanos vincere posse* (Ennius, Annals vi. 6) is 'I declare that you, descendant of Aeacus, can conquer the Romans', though the possibility of taking *te* as the object and *Romanos* as the subject creates an ambiguity.

Another usage of habitual order that is common to most Indo-European languages is that the dative proper precedes the accusative. This order of words is one of the means whereby a modern Englishman distinguishes a flexionless dative from a flexionless accusative in instances like 'God send the prince a better companion!' and 'God send the companion a better prince!' (Shakespeare, Henry IV, Part II, i. 2. 224 f.). Yet here, as elsewhere, the order of words only creates a presumption in favour of a certain interpretation of the sentence. It would obviously be impossible to lay down a hard and fast rule that where a sentence has two objects, the one that comes first must be a dative. The accusative precedes the dative in sentences of the type 'Give it him', 'Tell it me'; or the two objects may both be accusatives, as in 'I asked the boy a question'. Thus the order of words is never more than an auxiliary agency in indicating the meaning. This clue is unnecessary in Greek and Latin, because the dative always differs in form from the accusative in these languages; yet the dative habitually stands before the accusative, e.g. Λυσίας ἀνέθηκεν Ἀθηναίᾳ ἀπαρχήν, *Cicero Lentulo salutem dicit*.

(ii) *Context.* The effect of the environment or setting of a form in determining its case is seen in instances like *Filiae meae carmina Tibulli recito.* Here it is the contrast of the genitive *Tibulli* that shows *filiae meae* to be a dative; if *Tibulli* were omitted, *filiae meae* would naturally be taken as a genitive. The far-reaching effects of the context in distinguishing the cases of words may be illustrated by an amusing instance. The poem called *Des Deutschen Vaterland*, 'The German's Fatherland', written by the German patriot, E. M. Arndt, in 1813—a passionate appeal for a United Germany—contains the following lines:

> So weit die deutsche Zunge klingt
> Und Gott im Himmel Lieder singt,
> Das soll es sein!
> Das, wackrer Deutscher, nenne dein!

An English or an American reader might be excused for taking these lines at their face value—'Wherever the German tongue is spoken and God sings songs in Heaven, that shall be the Fatherland'—and feeling a mild surprise at the magnitude of the poet's claim and his anthropomorphic conception of the Deity. The word 'Gott' is, of course, a dative; but it is not shown to be such by its form, and the order of words does not exclude the possibility of its being taken as a nominative. What proves it to be a dative is simply the fact that in this context the dative is the only case that makes sense: 'Wherever the German tongue is spoken and sings (i.e. wherever speakers of German sing) hymns to God in heaven'.

(iii) The effect of *phrasing and intonation* in distinguishing cases may be illustrated by the special tone in which sentences containing vocatives are uttered in modern languages—the vocative being also separated off from the rest of the sentence by a pause[1]. Contrast 'Man! know thyself' with 'This man knows himself'; and 'I love thee still, my country!' (Cowper) with 'I love my country', or 'I love England, my native land', where *land* stands in apposition to *England*. How far this agency may be employed to distinguish other case-relations it is difficult

---

[1] There is evidence that the vocative, when it stood at the beginning of a sentence or a line of verse, had a special intonation in Vedic; and probably something of the same kind might be said of Greek and Latin.

to say with confidence. But it is an instrument of uncanny subtlety, whose uses go much farther than we consciously realize, even in our own language.

§ 12. If, then, variation of form is only one of four agencies whereby distinctions of case may be indicated, it is illogical to say that cases cannot exist in the absence of distinctive forms. The form of a case need not be either inflected or distinctive, as we have seen (§ 2). In the Germanic languages, ancient as well as modern (especially English), there are comparatively few surviving inflexions, most of them having been obliterated by processes of phonetic change[1]. But the uninflected form of a modern English noun without a preposition (e.g. 'man') is used in much the same ways as the nominative, the vocative, the accusative, and the dative of Latin nouns, and may be described as being any one of these cases according to its function in the sentence in which it stands. Just as many English words may belong to different parts of speech according to their functions in particular sentences (e.g. 'love' or 'face' or 'man' may be either a noun or a verb, 'black' either an adjective or a noun or a verb, 'long' and 'slow' either an adjective or an adverb), so the uninflected form of an English noun may belong to different cases[2]. The formal difference between modern English and modern German is only a difference of degree; so too the greater formal difference between modern English and Greek or Latin.

[1] It is misleading to speak of modern English as having 'discarded' its inflexions. What has really happened is that most of the distinctive forms of nouns and verbs have come to coincide in modern English, owing to the cumulative effects of a succession of minute sound-changes. For example, it is simply by the gradual operation of certain well-established phonetic laws that the inflected nominative and accusative singular of the parent language (seen in the Latin *lupu-s, lupu-m* and in the Greek λύκο-s, λύκο-ν) coincide in the Anglo-Saxon *wulf* and the modern English *wolf*. The reconstructed forms of the nominative and the accusative singular of the word meaning 'wolf' in the parent language are represented by the symbols *u̯l̥qu̯o-s* and *u̯l̥qu̯o-m* (Brugmann, K. V. Gr. §§ 454, 458).

[2] Similarly identical sounds may constitute different words, e.g. 'serial' and 'cereal'. Jespersen himself recognizes that 'long' and 'slow' may belong to two different parts of speech (Phil. of Gram. p. 52).

The term 'case' is necessary at some stage in the teaching of English itself—apart from its relation to other languages of the Indo-European family. This is admitted by all the schools of grammarians mentioned in § 8. They differ only in regard to the *number* of cases to be recognized in English, and how they are to be named. These differences ultimately depend on how the term 'case' is defined.

Let us ask, then, how it has come about that some grammarians have restricted the application of the term to distinctive forms. The answer is probably twofold. In the first place they failed to see that a form may stand in a relation to another member of a sentence without itself showing that relation—the relation being shown by agencies other than form (§ 11). In the second place there has been a not unnatural temptation to assume that the forms of the cases in highly inflected languages must have been *originally* distinct from one another, however much they may have come to coincide at a later date. But this assumption is not really warranted by what is known of the early stages in the history of the Indo-European languages, as can easily be proved.

§ 13. The parent language of this family, as reconstructed by comparative grammarians, had eight (or, as some say, nine) cases:

  (i) a nominative⎫
 (ii) a vocative   ⎬ used mainly as in the daughter languages;
(iii) an accusative⎭

 (iv) a dative, limited to the meanings which are expressible by the English 'to' or 'for' (as used to form a dative-equivalent[1]), and never joined with a preposition[2];

 (v) a genitive, limited to meanings which are expressible by the English 'of';

---

[1] In Hindustani these meanings are generally expressed by the same word, viz. the postposition *ko*.

[2] In Vedic and Sanskrit the dative is thus restricted.

(vi) an ablative, limited to meanings which are expressible by the English 'from';

(vii) a locative, expressing the meaning of 'at' or 'in';

(viii) a sociative-instrumental, expressing the meaning of 'with'; this case is regarded by some grammarians as two cases, on the ground of the difference of meaning between accompaniment and instrumentality.

But these eight cases were not all different in form. To mention only a few instances, (*a*) all neuters of whatever declension had the same form in the nominative, the vocative, and the accusative cases (singular and plural), as in Greek and Latin; (*b*) the genitive and the ablative were identical in form in the singular number, except in one declension (that of the *o*-stems, which formed the ablative by means of the suffix *d*); (*c*) in the plural and dual numbers the dative and the ablative had the same forms throughout, as in Latin; (*d*) the sociative and the instrumental, if these are to be regarded as two distinct cases, were identical in form throughout.

And, conversely, the same case often had several different forms: for example, the nominative singular was formed sometimes with the suffix *s*, sometimes without any suffix; compare the Greek λύκο-ς, ὁδού-ς and the Latin *lupu-s, den-s* with the Greek ὥρα, πατήρ and the Latin *hora, pater*. The genitive singular was formed in several different ways, so that the parent language had side by side genitives which were morphologically as heterogeneous as the Greek ὥρα-ς, κυν-ός, λύκου, λύκοιο and the Latin *familia-s, can-is, lupi*. But the most remarkable instances of diversity of form in identical cases are due to the fact that in the dual and plural numbers the cases were formed quite otherwise than in the singular number. It is due to this peculiarity in the parent language of our family that in Greek the genitive of ὥρα is in the singular ὥρας, but in the dual ὥραιν and in the plural ὡρῶν, and that in Latin the genitive of *hora* is in the singular *horae*, but in the plural *horarum*. We are so familiar with this feature of the Indo-European languages that we regard it as a matter of course; yet there is no logical reason why the case-inflexions of the dual and the plural should

be different from those of the singular. For the case-relations
are the same whether we are speaking of one or of more than
one person or thing[1].

The facts mentioned in this paragraph demonstrate conclu-
sively that the principle of 'one case, one form' has only a very
limited application to the parent language or to the daughter
languages of our family; it might, indeed, almost be said to be
more honoured in the breach than in the observance.

§ 14. But what is the explanation of the fact that the eight or
nine cases of the parent language are represented by only six
cases in Latin and only five in Greek and the Germanic
languages? The answer is that this was the result of a process
of amalgamation or fusing of cases, called 'syncretism'. By this
process two or more cases, having points of contact in form or
in meaning, were unified in a single composite case, which
combined under a common form the functions of two or more
cases of the parent language. Thus in Greek (i) the genitive and
the ablative, which were already partly identical in form (§ 13 b),
were amalgamated throughout; and (ii) the dative, the locative,
and the sociative-instrumental were united in a single case. These
resultant composite cases are rightly called 'genitive' and 'dative'
respectively, because the old genitive and the old dative remained
the predominant partners in the new genitive and the new dative.
But it is important to recognize clearly that the Greek genitive
and the Greek dative were only partially coincident in meaning
with the genitive and the dative of the parent language. Each
of these Greek cases had acquired an enlarged sphere of meaning;
the genitive had become an *of-from* case, the dative a *to(for)-at*
(*in*)-*with* case. These different meanings, however, were not

[1] In some languages of other families the oblique cases are formed by
means of the same suffixes in the plural as in the singular, for example in
Turkish, where the same suffixes *i, ín, é, dén, dé* form (respectively) the
accusative, the genitive, the dative, the ablative, and the locative in both
numbers: thus *ev* 'house' forms the genitive *ev-ín*, and *evler* 'houses'
forms the genitive *evler-ín*. In Hungarian the singular *katona* 'soldier' and
the plural *katonak* 'soldiers' both form the genitive by adding the same
suffix: *katona-nak, katonak-nak*. This feature is reproduced in Esperanto,
e.g. *mi vidas arbo-n* 'I see a tree', *mi vidas arboj-n* 'I see trees'.

indistinguishably confused; they lay side by side, but were distinguishable, though not always distinguished. Thus in the
Greek genitive two distinct strands of meaning can be recognized
—that of the genitive proper (i.e. the genitive of the parent
language) and that of the ablatival genitive; and in the Greek
dative we can recognize three distinct strands of meaning—that
of the dative proper, that of the locatival dative, and that of the
sociative-instrumental dative.

The Latin ablative is a strange conglomerate of elements
derived from three distinct sources—the ablative proper, the
locative, and the sociative-instrumental of the parent language.
Thus the number of cases was reduced in Latin to six. But
this sixth Latin case (called 'ablative') had in the process of
amalgamation become a *from-at-with* case, by no means identical
with the ablative of the parent language. That the name 'ablative'
was inadequate as a description of this three-headed Latin case
was recognized by at least one of the Roman grammarians.
Quintilian, in his Institutes of Oratory (I. 4. 26), makes or
quotes the acute remark that an intelligent teacher should enquire
whether a seventh case ought not to be recognized in Latin, and
a sixth in Greek:—"For when I say *hasta percussi*, I am not
using an ablative proper (*non utor ablativi natura*), and when I
express the same idea in Greek I am not using a dative proper".
Here Quintilian or his authority really anticipated one of the
results of modern comparative grammar: he had noticed that
in the Latin ablative and the Greek dative another case (the
instrumental) was concealed. This passage is also interesting as
showing that the names of the cases were to a Roman grammarian
functional, not morphological, terms[1].

---

[1] This passage clearly disproves Prof. Jespersen's confident statement
that no one would have dreamt of postulating a Latin ablative case if it
had not in many instances been different in form from the dative (*op. cit.*
p. 177). Here we have a Roman grammarian dreaming of an instrumental
case, identical in form with the ablative but differing from it in meaning.
Some of the later Roman grammarians went further and actually set up a
septimus casus in forma ablativi. It was, then, clearly possible for an ancient
grammarian to recognize distinctions of case in the absence of distinctions
of form.

§ 15. In the Germanic languages—a term which of course includes English—the dative, the ablative, the locative, and the sociative-instrumental cases of the parent language were ultimately welded into one composite case, called the dative, which thus came to be used in indicating four incongruous relations—those of 'from' and 'in' and 'with', as well as that of the dative proper ('to' or 'for')[1]. The Germanic dative, in fact, came to have an even wider range of meaning than the Latin ablative. In the old Germanic languages ablatival, locatival, and sociative-instrumental datives were widely used without a preposition[2]; but in modern German they are found only in phrases formed with a preposition, such as *aus dem Hause, in dem Hause, mit meinen Freunden*. Such datives are not datives proper; for *aus dem Hause* can never have meant 'out to-the-house', or 'out for-the-house'; it meant from the first 'out *from*-the-house', i.e. the dative was ablatival, corresponding to the meaning of the preposition *aus*; in examples like *in dem Hause* the dative was locatival, in examples like *mit meinen Freunden* it was sociative. The meanings of these datives improper are, no doubt, overshadowed in the consciousness of the modern German by the meanings which are inherent in the prepositions themselves.

---

[1] This paragraph supplies the historical justification for the procedure of the British and the American Terminology Committees in not including an ablative in the list of modern English cases or case-uses. This exclusion of the ablative has been criticized by Prof. Allen Mawer (The Problem of Grammar, p. 13) and Prof. Jespersen (*op. cit.* p. 177) as needing justification. These critics ought to have seen that the terminology committees were not engaged on the task of imposing the Latin case-system upon English, but were simply recognizing the well-known fact that certain of the cases belonging to the Indo-European case-system have not survived as separate cases in modern English. The use of *names* of Latin origin for the five English cases does not in the least involve the forcing of the Latin case-system upon English.

[2] For example, in Gothic *maiza imma* 'greater than he' ($=\mu\epsilon i\zeta\omega\nu \ a\dot{v}\tau o\hat{v}$, Matth. xi. 11), and in Anglo-Saxon *him betera* 'better than he' (ablatival datives of comparison); in Gothic *naht jah daga* 'by night and by day', and in Old High German *thritten tage* 'on the third day' (locatival datives); in Anglo-Saxon *tryddode getrume micle* 'he came with a great troop', and *he geendode yflum deaþe* 'he ended with an evil death' (sociative datives).

Nevertheless these datives convey *something* to his mind—an idea distinct from that of the accusative; this is at any rate clear in the familiar usage of different cases with the same preposition according as the verb of the sentence denotes rest at or motion towards a place. The prepositions admitting this twofold construction are *an, auf, hinter, in, neben, über, unter, vor,* and *zwischen,* e.g. *in dem Hause wohnen,* but *in das Haus gehen.* In modern English the sense of a distinction between datives improper and accusatives has been lost, partly because the distinction of form between the two cases has been obliterated by phonetic change, partly because Anglo-Saxon usage was not consistent with itself; see § 69. The only datives that are recognizable as such in modern English are datives proper, and even these only in contexts in which they can be replaced by phrases formed with 'to' or 'for'[1].

§ 16. The above account of 'syncretism' explains the fact that the number of cases is not the same in all the languages of our family. It must, however, be added that isolated instances of the survival of some of the original cases (*not* amalgamated with other cases) occur in several languages. For instance, we find a few survivals of the original locative in Greek and Latin: e.g. οἴκοι 'at home', Ἰσθμοῖ 'at the Isthmus', Ἀθήνησι 'in Athens', *domi* 'at home', *vesperi* 'in the evening', *Ephesi, Romae,* etc. These are locatives both in meaning and in form. In modern English we have a survival of the old sociative-instrumental (*not*

[1] Jespersen's strange denial of the existence of any truly grammatical criterion, either of form or of function, whereby a dative can be distinguished from an accusative in modern English (see above, note on p. 8) is due to his neglect of the distinction which has been so clearly established by comparative grammarians between datives proper and those datives improper—the ghosts of departed ablatives, locatives, and sociative-instrumentals—which have found an abode in the Germanic dative but have no proper datival meaning. To Jespersen all datives seem to belong to one and the same grammatical category—a category in which various meanings are indistinguishably confused: "The meaning of the dative in those languages which possess it is vague and indistinct from a notional point of view" (*op. cit.* p. 178). This is not true of the Latin dative at any rate, and it is also untrue of the dative proper in the other languages of our family.

amalgamated with the dative) in the word *the* when it denotes the measure of difference, as in '*the* more, *the* merrier', 'I am all *the* more inclined to help him'. The Anglo-Saxon form of this word was *thē* or *thȳ* (not the same as the dative *thǣm*).

§ 17. Few traces of the original *case-forms* survive in modern languages; for the distinctive forms of the cases—where they had distinctive forms—have to a great extent come to coincide owing to processes of phonetic change (§ 12, note). This levelling of case-forms is very noticeable in all the modern languages of our family, including the modern Indo-Aryan languages. In modern Greek the distinctive form of the dative has disappeared. In modern German some of the inflexions of case that survived in the old Germanic languages have disappeared; for example, all feminine nouns are now uninflected in the singular number. In modern English this process has gone still further: we retain only the inflexion of the genitive in nouns (e.g. *man's*, *men's*) and two case-forms of certain personal pronouns (*I*, *me*; *thou*, *thee*; *he*, *him*; etc.). But the disappearance of distinctive case-forms does not involve the disappearance of cases, if the term 'case' is defined as in § 9. The uninflected form of a modern English noun (e.g. *man*) is used *without a preposition* in much the same ways as the forms (partly inflected, partly uninflected) of the old Germanic nominative, vocative, accusative, and dative proper; and the inflected form (e.g. *man's*) in much the same way as the old Germanic genitive[1].

In modern French and Spanish all the distinctive case-forms of nouns have disappeared, including that of the genitive, which is replaced by a phrase formed with *de*. But some of the case-forms of personal pronouns have survived.

§ 18. We are now in a position to map out the cases as they came to be in English, German, Latin, French, Spanish, and Greek, subsequently to the processes of development which have been sketched above. (See Table, p. 21.)

[1] The modern English uninflected form enters into no *new* case-relations; the only relations in which it stands *fall within* the groups of relations in which the old inflected forms stood.

NOMINATIVE	
VOCATIVE ACCUSATIVE DATIVE PROPER } in all the six languages, §§ 20–45	
	DATIVES IMPROPER (in German and Greek, §§ 46–48)
GENITIVE PROPER (in English, German, Latin, Greek, §§ 49–52)	GENITIVE IMPROPER (in Greek, § 53)
ABLATIVE PROPER (in Latin, §§ 54, 55)	ABLATIVES IMPROPER (in Latin, §§ 56, 57)

§ 19. In the sequel we shall consider first the uses of these cases without prepositions, reserving their use with prepositions for later treatment (under the head of *Case-phrases*, §§ 65 ff.). The usages which are common to all these six languages are printed in a larger size of type and distinguished by a marginal line. It can thus be seen at a glance how much of the domain of each case is the common property of all the six languages, and how much of it is not.

The examples are given in the following order: ENGLISH, GERMAN, LATIN, FRENCH, SPANISH, GREEK. The examples in each section are intended to be read as supplementing one another: an example in one language is generally to be taken as representing a similar expression in the other languages.

USES OF THE NOMINATIVE

§ 20. The nominative is used as the subject of a sentence or clause, and predicatively of the subject:

England expects that every *man* will do his duty.— Are *you* not *he*, *that* frights the maidens of the villagery?

Ein unnütz *Leben* ist ein früher *Tod*.—*Was* ist des Deutschen *Vaterland*?

Roma totius orbis terrarum *caput* fuit.

*J'*y suis et *j'*y reste.—Le *secret* d'ennuyer est *celui* de tout dire.

Quien [*El que*] sabe eso sabe mucho.—*Lo* que he dicho es *verdad*.

Ἔσσεται ἦμαρ ὅτ᾽ ἄν ποτ᾽ ὀλώλῃ Ἴλιος ἱρή.

For passive constructions with the nominative see § 24.

§ 21. In modern French (since the sixteenth century) 'tonic' forms of personal pronouns, derived from oblique cases pronounced with a stress, are used as nominatives in instances like 'Qui est là? *Moi*', '*Moi*, je le sais; *toi*, tu ne le sais pas', 'C'est *moi* [*toi, lui*]', 'Ce sont *eux*'.

USES OF THE VOCATIVE

§ 22. The vocative, which in the parent language was formed without any case-suffix and in the daughter languages is generally identical in form with the nominative, may stand in either of two relations to the rest of the sentence:

(i) It may denote the person or personified thing addressed:

England, awake!—Nobody asked you, *sir*, she said.

O *du Deutschland*, ich muss marschieren.

Audi, *Iuppiter*!—Audi *tu*, *populus* Albanus[1].—Da, meus *ocellus*, mea *rosa*, mi *anime*, mea *voluptas, Leonida*, argentum mihi[2].

---

[1] *Populus* is here (Livy i. 24. 7) a vocative, not a nominative. There was no distinctive vocatival form of this word in classical Latin, i.e. the form *popule* was not used: cf. Ovid, Fasti iv. 731.

[2] Plautus, Asin. 664: *ocellus* and *anime* are both vocatives.

Tu l'as voulu, *George Dandin*, tu l'as voulu.
Ven aquí, *tú.*—Bien vengas, *mal*, si vienes solo.
Τέτλαθι δή, κραδίη· καὶ κύντερον ἄλλο ποτ᾽ ἔτλης.

(ii) It may denote a person or personified thing invoked,
but not addressed:

Good *God*, is that you?
Donnerwetter, wie fängt er das an?
Iuppiter, estne istic Charinus?—Scelestum, *di immor-*
tales, et nefarium facinus!
Ah! *diable*! je n'y pensais pas.
¿Qué *diablos* hacer?—¿Cómo *diablos* puede ser eso?
ὠκβάτανα, τοῦ σχήματος (Aristophanes, Ach. 64).

USES OF THE ACCUSATIVE WITHOUT
A PREPOSITION

§ 23. The accusative without a preposition has a twofold use:

(i) **As an object,** denoting that which is affected or
effected by the verbal activity, and predicatively of the
object:

Who steals. my *purse* steals *trash*; but he that filches
from me my good *name* robs *me* of that which not
enriches *him.*—He called *me* an *ass.*
Die Vögel bauen ihre *Nester.*—Keinen *Reimer* wird
man finden, der sich nicht den *besten* hält (Goethe).
Romani *Quintum Fabium* 'cunctatorem' appellabant.
Ses amis *l'*estiment.—Qui *s'*excuse *s'*accuse.
Quien *te* cubre, *te* descubre (Don Quixote).—Buen
corazón quebranta mala *ventura* (Don Quixote).
Ψευδωνύμως σε δαίμονες Προμηθέα καλοῦσιν.

Cognate objects:

To live a blameless *life*.
Den *Heldentod* sterben.
Mirum *somnium* somniare.
Danser une *contredanse*.
Dormir la *siesta*.
Βίον ἀνθρώπινον ζῆν—ναυμαχίαν νικᾶν.

§ 24. In the passive inversion of these constructions (§ 23) accusatives become nominatives (§ 20):

Purses are stolen daily.
Nester werden von Vögeln gebaut.
Quintus Fabius 'cunctator' a Romanis appellabatur.
Il est estimé de ses amis.
César fué matado por Bruto.
Καλοῦμαι Προμηθεύς.

§ 25. Some English, German, Latin, and Greek verbs take two objects, both in the accusative, the one denoting a person affected, the other a thing effected or affected, by the verbal activity:

He asked *me* a *question* [a *favour*, my *opinion*, etc.].
Ich frage [bitte] *dich eins.*—Ich lehre *dich* die englische *Sprache.*
Hoc te interrogo [rogo].—Romani *Nervios haec* docebant.
Ἐρωτᾷς με τὸ ὄνομα [τὴν γνώμην].—Βασιλεὺς ὑμᾶς τὰ ὅπλα ἀπαιτεῖ.—Οἱ Πέρσαι διδάσκουσι τοὺς παῖδας σωφροσύνην.

§ 26. In the passive inversion of this construction the accusative denoting the person becomes the subject of the sentence, and the accusative denoting the thing is retained (though the verb is passive):

I am asked a *question* [a *favour*, my *opinion*].
Du wirst *Englisch* gelehrt. (Rare in modern German.)
Sententiam rogatus est.—*Nervii haec* a Romanis docebantur.
Ἐρωτῶμαι τὸ ὄνομα [τὴν γνώμην].—Οἱ παῖδες διδάσκονται σωφροσύνην ὑπὸ τῶν Περσῶν.

§ 27. Out of sentences containing two objects sprang a construction of great importance, **the accusative with the infinitive** (equivalent to a subordinate clause in a complex sentence). The germ of the construction is seen in sentences like the following, in which the accusative and the infinitive are two separate objects of the governing verb:

I saw *him die.*
Ich hörte die *Vögel singen.*
Audivi *classicum canere.*
On entendait *bourdonner* l'*abeille.*
Los vi *caer* [*morir*].

In sentences like the following the accusative has coalesced with the infinitive into a single object, in which the infinitive has acquired predicative meaning and the accusative has become its subject:

I believe *him to be* an honest man (= that he is an honest man).
Sie weiss *mich* in Wüsten *irren* (Schiller).—Du wähnst *dich* klug *zu sein* (Platen)[1].
Arbitror *eum esse* virum probum.
Nous habitons une ville *que* l'on dit *être* la plus belle du monde[2].
Esta ciudad *que* dicen *ser* una maravilla[2].—La venta *que* él imaginaba *ser* castillo (Don Quixote).
Νομίζω αὐτὸν εἶναι ἄνδρα χρηστόν: cf. Οἶδα ὅτι ἀνὴρ χρηστός ἐστιν.

§ 28. (ii) **As an adverbial qualification** the accusative without a preposition properly denotes either direction

[1] The construction was well established in several of the old Germanic languages (Anglo-Saxon, Gothic, and Old High German). But in German of the present day it is obsolete. Examples are occasionally found in Luther, Lessing, Herder, Goethe, Schiller, Tieck, and other writers of the sixteenth to the nineteenth centuries.

[2] In modern French and Spanish the construction is used only when the accusative is a relative pronoun.

in space (*whither*) or extension in space or time (*how far*
or *how long*):

> Go *home*.—I have walked twenty *miles*.—They sat an
> *hour* [all *day*, five *days*] in council[1].
> Ich bin zehn *Stunden* gegangen [geblieben].
> Abi *domum* [*rus*, *Romam*].—Viginti *milia* passuum
> [totum *diem*] ambulavi.—Abhinc *annos* duos ('two
> years ago').—Aliquot ante *annos* ('several years be-
> fore').—*Quartum* post *diem* ('the fourth day after'
> = four days afterwards).—Ante *diem quartum* Nonas
> Ianuarias ('the fourth day before the nones of Janu-
> ary'); here the adverb *ante*, qualified by *diem quartum*,
> acts as a preposition governing the accusative *Nonas*[2].
> Elle a régné plusieurs *ans*.—Votre affaire ne marche
> *pas* (lit. 'does not progress a step').—Je n'irai *point*
> (lit. 'I shall not go a point').
> Hemos andado tres *leguas*.—Vivió cuarenta *años* en
> Lisboa.
> Οἶκον ἐλεύσεται (Homer, Od. xix. 313).—Κνίσῃ
> οὐρανὸν ἷκεν (Il. i. 317).—Μύρια στάδια ἐπορεύ-
> θησαν.

§ 29. Freer uses of the adverbial accusative:

(i) Denoting time when:

> Er kommt den *sechsten* November.—Er arbeitet jeden
> *Tag*.—*Id* temporis mortuus est ('at that time').—
> Qu'est-ce qu'il deviendra un *jour*?—Salimos el *lunes*.

---

[1] In Anglo-Saxon the case used in such expressions as these was the
accusative, e.g. *hām* 'homewards'. The modern English 'home' is a slightly
changed form of the same word.

[2] This explanation of the construction was offered in The Gateway to
Latin Composition (Oxford, 1924, p. 203), and also in the same year by
Wackernagel in his Vorlesungen über Syntax, Zweite Reihe, p. 195.

Τὴν ὥραν σπείρειν ('to sow at the right time', Xen. Oecon. 17. 1).—Τὴν ἡμέραν τῆς πεντηκοστῆς ('on the day of Pentecost', Acts xx. 16).

(ii) In other adverbial expressions:

Er führte mich einen andern *Weg*.—Es ist keinen *Heller* werth.—*Multum* [*Nihil*] valet.—Decem *libras* pondo valet.—Maximam *partem* lacte vivunt.—Il est *beaucoup* (from Low Latin *colpum*) plus savant.—Vale tres *duros*.—Pesa dos *arrobas*.—Πάντ᾽ εὐδαιμονεῖ.

In the light of these developments of the adverbial accusative the corresponding modern English expressions may be regarded as containing accusatives, even in instances in which the case used in Anglo-Saxon was the dative or the genitive. For in all the languages of our family the accusative has encroached upon the domains of other cases. For example, instead of πολλῷ μείζων 'greater by much' (§ 46. v) the Greeks sometimes said πολὺ μείζων.

USES OF THE DATIVE WITHOUT A PREPOSITION

I. THE DATIVE PROPER

§ 30. All Latin, French, and Spanish datives are datives proper; but in French and Spanish the dative is limited to personal pronouns: instead of the dative of nouns these languages use a phrase formed with a preposition (French *à*, Spanish *a*), which is equivalent to a dative and may therefore be called a dative-phrase. The case used in these phrases is not a dative; for no preposition ever takes a dative in Latin or the languages descended from Latin.

§ 31. In modern English the dative proper of both nouns and pronouns is quite common; but it can be distinguished from the accusative only by the context in which it stands and by the order of words (§ 11. i, ii and § 15, end).

§ 32. The dative proper has three uses: (i) as an indirect object, (ii) as an adverbial qualification of a verb or an adjective, (iii) occasionally as an adjectival qualification of a noun or a pronoun.

§ 33. (i) The verbs that take the dative as an **indirect object** are for the most part of similar meaning in all the languages of our family:

He caused his *father* much anxiety.—Give [Pay] *me* the money.—Tell *him* the truth.—Write *me* a letter about the matter.

Dem *Tell* verdank' ich mein gerettet Leben.—Ueberlass *mir* diese Sache.

Carthaginiensibus tributum imperaverunt ('They imposed tribute upon the Carthaginians').—Divitias *mihi* invidet.

Je *vous* raconterai l'histoire.—Il le *lui* présenta.—Il *leur* apprend le français (cf. § 25).

Quien *te* da un hueso, no te quiere ver muerto (Don Quixote).—*Les* he prestado mi libro.—Dispénse*me* V. la molestia que *le* causo.—Enséñan*les* artes (cf. § 25).
Ξενοφῶντι τὴν ἀρχὴν ἐπιτρέπουσιν.

§ 34. Some of these verbs may take as their direct object an infinitive or a clause, in place of the accusative:

I told him *to come.*—He promised [wrote] me *that he would come.*

Erzähle mir *was geschehen ist.*

Impera iis *ut veniant.*

Je lui demanderai *de venir.*

Les prometieron *cantar.*

Τοῖς ναύταις παραινῶ μὴ ἐκπεπλῆχθαι.

§ 35. In the passive inversion the accusative-object generally becomes the subject of the sentence :

The *money* was paid me.

Diese *Sache* ist mir überlassen worden.

Tributum Carthaginiensibus imperatum est.

Le *chemin* m'a été montré.

El *camino* me fué mostrado.

Ξενοφῶντι ἡ ἀρχὴ ἐπιτρέπεται.

But in English, in Greek, and occasionally in Latin the dative-object may become the subject, the accusative-object being retained (cf. § 26):

I was shown the *way*.—*We* were offered a large *sum* of money.—*He* was awarded the *prize*.—*They* were forbidden the *house* [debarred the *freedom* of the air].—*He* was told *to come*.

Ξενοφῶν ἐπιτρέπεται τὴν ἀρχήν.—Δέλτος ἐγγεγραμμένη ξυνθήματα ('A tablet having tokens inscribed upon it', Sophocles, Trach. 157).

Flores inscripti *nomina* regum ('Flowers having the names of kings inscribed on them', Virgil, Ecl. iii. 106).—Haec *ego procurare* imperor (Horace, Epist. i. 5. 21).

§ 36. Verbs taking the dative proper as sole object :

(*a*) In instances like the following an accusative-object may be supplied :

Won't you tell *me* [pay *me*, pardon *me*] ?—I will write *you* about the matter.

Ich danke *dir* (cf. 'Dir danke ich mein ganzes Glück', with two objects).—Sprich *mir* von Orest (Goethe).

Mihi invidet.—*Mihi* crede [ignosce].—*Servo* meo impero.

Dieu *me* pardonne! (cf. 'Puisse le public me pardonner mes fautes!').

Dispénse*me*.

Εἰπέ μοι.—Σύγγνωθι ἡμῖν.—Πτωχὸς πτωχῷ φθονεῖ.

(*b*) In instances like the following no accusative can be supplied. The verbs that take this construction have a close affinity of meaning—verbs of 'benefiting', 'injuring', 'pleasing', 'displeasing', 'obeying', 'resisting', and the like. But in modern English the case depending on such verbs is no longer distinguishable from an accusative (cf. § 15, end)[1]:

Er schadet *uns* und nützt [hilft] *sich* nicht.
Illud *mihi* placet [displicet].—Venus *Volcano* nupsit[2].
Je *lui* obéis.—Tout le monde *lui* résistera.
A quien Dios quiere, su casa *le* sabe (Don Quixote).
Μαντικῇ οὐ πείθομαι [πιστεύω].—Ἕπεσθέ μοι.

§ 37. The passive inversion of these constructions (§ 36 *a* and *b*), where possible at all, is ordinarily expressed by an impersonal passive construction in German and Latin: Mir wird geholfen.— Mihi invidetur. But in French and Spanish an active construction is generally substituted: On lui pardonnera.—Les pesaba la muerte del amigo. In Greek the same passive construction is employed as with verbs that take an accusative-object (§ 24), i.e. the dative of the active construction becomes the subject of the passive (cf. § 35): Πένης λέγων τἀληθὲς οὐ πιστεύεται.

§ 38. (ii) As an **adverbial qualification**, denoting the person or thing interested or concerned, the dative proper is found (*a*) with verbs, §§ 39-43, (*b*) with adjectives and adverbs, § 44.

§ 39. (*a*) *Adverbial datives with verbs :*

He has built *me* [*himself*] a house.—They saddled *him* the ass (1 Kings xiii. 13).—Write *me* out that lesson.—Keep *me* a good seat.—I wish *you* a Happy New Year.

---

[1] In Anglo-Saxon such verbs took the dative, e.g. *mannum derian* 'to injure men'.

[2] *Nubo* means literally 'I am united in marriage'; it is connected with νύμφη 'bride', and has nothing to do with *ob-nubo* in the sense of veiling. Some Latin dative-verbs are also found with an accusative object, e.g. Di *vos* benefaciant (C. I. L. vi. 2335); so *parco* (Plautus, Curc. 381), *studeo* (Mil. 1437), *medeor* (Terence, Phorm. 822), etc.

Er hat *sich* viel Geld verdient.—Man hat *mir* alles genommen ('for me' = from me).

Non *tibi* ipsi sed toti *reipublicae* vivis.—Compedes *tibi* adimam ('for you' = from you; Plautus, Capt. 1028). Je *me* suis acheté des gants[1].—Il *leur* a pris toutes ses marchandises ('for them' = from them).—Je *lui* ai arraché une dent.

Me lavaba las manos[1].—*Se* ha roto el brazo.—*Te* deseo feliz año nuevo.—*Me* quitaron el reloj ('for me' = from me).

Πᾶς ἀνὴρ αὑτῷ πονεῖ.—Τοῖσιν ἀφείλετο νόστιμον ἦμαρ ('for them' = from them; Homer).

§ 40. Adverbial datives differ from datives of the indirect object (§ 33) in that they cannot become the subject of a passive construction. The only possible passive construction of such sentences as the above (§ 39) is that in which the accusative becomes the subject of the passive verb: e.g. A *house* has been built *me* (= for me).—*Alles* ist *mir* genommen worden.—*Compedes tibi* adimentur. But here too, as in § 37, French and Spanish prefer an active construction.

§ 41. The adverbial dative sometimes marks a person (often the speaker himself) as interested in or sympathizing with what is said in the rest of the sentence, rather than as concerned in the action spoken of. This is the so-called 'ethical' dative: it would be better called 'emotional' or 'pathetic':

Give *me* your present to one Master Bassanio (*me* = 'I beg you to do so'; Shakespeare, Merch. of Ven. ii. 2. 115).

---

[1] Here a dative-phrase with *à* (or *a*) could not be used as a substitute for the dative in French or Spanish.

Sieh *mir* nicht so finster aus ('Pray don't look so sullen').

At *tibi* repente venit ad me Caninius (*tibi* = you will be interested to hear).

Que *me* faites-vous là? (*me* = I should like to know).

Me han muerto a mi hijo (*me* adds an emotional touch).

Τοιοῦτο ὑμῖν ἐστιν ἡ τυραννίς, ὦ Λακεδαιμόνιοι (ὑμῖν = you may be surprised to hear).

§ 42. In Latin and Greek the adverbial dative with *esse* or εἶναι is used in two special senses:

Denoting possession:

Est *mihi* cadus vini ('There is for me' = I have).

Τὸ ὄνομα τῷ μειρακίῳ ἦν Πλάτων ('The young man had the name Plato').

Denoting the agent:

Hic *tibi* vitandus est ('He is for you a person to be avoided' = He must be avoided *by you*).

Ἡ ἀρετὴ πᾶσιν ἀσκητέα ἐστίν.

§ 43. In Latin the adverbial dative may be used predicatively to denote the end served:

Hoc mihi *solacio* est ('This is a consolation to me', 'Dies gereicht mir zum Troste').

Hoc tibi *laudi* sed aliis *vitio* duxisti ('You thought this a credit to yourself, but a discredit to others').

§ 44. (*b*) *Adverbial datives with adjectives and adverbs:*

You are like [unlike] *him*.—He sat near the *fire*.— Wear flannel next the *skin*.—We are nearer *home* to-day than we were yesterday.—Who comes nearest *him* in wit?—Opposite the *post-office* is a barber's shop.

These English cases are historically datives proper, and, as such, are replaceable by dative-phrases: e.g.

'liker *to God* than *to man*', 'nearer *to Thee*'[1]. In modern
English the only adjectives and adverbs that take
an adverbial dative are those that denote likeness and
nearness; but in German, Latin, French, Spanish, and
Greek all adjectives and adverbs that may be qualified
by a dative-phrase formed with 'to' or 'for' in English
may take a dative:

Er ist seinem *Vater* ähnlich [dem *Tode* nahe].

Locus *flumini* propinquus [*castris* idoneus] erat.

Cela ne *leur* est pas utile [agréable, nécessaire, fatal,
etc.].

Me es útil [agradable, necesario, fatal, etc.].

Ἐχθρὸς ἐλευθερίᾳ καὶ νόμοις ἐναντίος ἐστὶν ὁ
τύραννος.

§ 45. (iii) The use of the dative proper as an **adjectival qualification** of a noun is comparatively rare, though there is nothing
in the nature of the dative to prevent its being joined with a noun,
as with a verb or an adjective. In English, French, and Spanish
we get in dependence on a noun not a dative but a dative-phrase:
'obedience to the laws', 'watchmaker to H.M. the King', 'a
house for sale', 'poudre à canon', 'boîte aux lettres', 'cartas por
contestar', etc. So too in German for the most part, though expressions like 'Gehorsam *dem Gesetze*' (= gegen das Gesetz) are
not unknown. In Latin neither a phrase formed with a preposition nor a dative is ordinarily used in dependence on a noun;
nevertheless we find expressions like 'obtemperatio *legibus*',
'comes *Niso*' (Virg. Aen. ix. 223), 'decemviri *sacris faciundis*',
'remedium *aegris rebus*', 'pabulum *ovibus*', '*receptui* signum audire
non possumus' (Cicero, Phil. xiii. 7. 15). In Greek such datives
are not uncommon, side by side with phrases formed with a preposition (preceded by the article, as in αἱ πρὸς πόλεμον παρα-
σκευαί), e.g. δῶρον τῷ οἴκῳ, φιλία τοῖς Ἀθηναίοις, ἄναξ

---

[1] Sweet (New English Grammar, § 1992) points out that these datives
are direct descendants of Anglo-Saxon datives, e.g. *nēah þǣm fȳre* 'near
the fire'.

SSG   3

Θήβαις, γραμματεὺς τῇ βουλῇ. Expressions like ἧλοι ταῖς θύραις ('nails for the doors') occur often in Attic inscriptions.

II. DATIVES IMPROPER

§ 46. (A) *Sociative-Instrumental Datives* without a preposition are found in the old Germanic languages (§ 15) and in Greek (§ 14). These usages of the Greek dative need not be set forth in detail here: they may be classified as datives of (i) association, (ii) attendant circumstances, (iii) instrument and means, (iv) cause, conceived as that *by* which a result is brought about, (v) measure of difference, (vi) respect, i.e. that in respect of which—a use related to the locatival meaning of the case (§ 47).—Compare the parallel classification of the sociative-instrumental ablative in Latin (§ 56).

§ 47. (B) *Locatival Datives* without a preposition are found in the old Germanic languages (§ 15) and in Greek (§ 14). The Greek datives of this kind may be classified as

(i) Datives denoting 'place where', used in Homer: e.g. αἰθέρι ναίων—τόξ' ὤμοισιν ἔχων—ἀριπρεπέα Τρώεσσιν.

(ii) Datives denoting 'time when', used in Attic as well as Homeric Greek: e.g. ταύτῃ τῇ ἡμέρᾳ—τῷ πέμπτῳ ἔτει.

§ 48. (C) *Ablatival Datives* without a preposition are found only in the old Germanic languages (§ 15).

USES OF THE GENITIVE WITHOUT A PREPOSITION

I. THE GENITIVE PROPER

§ 49. The genitive proper was inherited from the parent language by all the languages of the Indo-European family. But in French and Spanish it has been for the most part replaced by a phrase formed with a preposition (*de*), which is equivalent to a genitive and may therefore be called a genitive-phrase[1]. In modern English

---

[1] It is for this reason that the following paragraphs on the genitive contain no French or Spanish examples and no large type or marginal line. The uses of the French *en* and *dont* as equivalent to genitives are hardly worth special mention in this connexion. Where no English example is

too the old inflected genitive in -*s* is very often replaced by the genitive-phrase formed with 'of'; but it is by no means extinct. On the contrary, it is widely used with certain classes of nouns, and in some instances it is the *only* correct mode of expression, e.g. 'Mary's hat', 'a boys' book' (= a book for boys), 'the war's delays', 'a night's rest'. Moreover there is a distinct tendency at the present day to extend the use of the genitive: expressions like 'a nation's policy', 'Sweden's plans', 'on Oxford's part', 'September's bad start' are becoming quite common; e.g. "Faith's increase is assured when we loyally use what we have of its gifts" (The Times, March 5, 1927—'Saturday's Times').

§ 50. All the genitives found in English, German, and Latin, and most of those found in Greek, are genitives proper.

§ 51. The genitive proper has a very wide range of meaning: its uses comprise all the relations in which a noun or pronoun may be regarded as 'belonging to' or 'connected with' or 'falling within the sphere of' that which is denoted by some other word in the sentence (noun, adjective, or verb). The particular meanings which the genitive proper assumes in particular contexts are merely special aspects of this general meaning.

§ 52. One very important use of the genitive proper is as an adjectival qualification of a noun. But this is not necessarily the *earliest* use of the case. Its uses with adjectives and verbs are closely akin to its uses with nouns and may be treated side by side with them:

(i) **Possessive genitives,** denoting 'owned by':

Shakespeare*'s* house—*England's* greatest son.
Goethes Vater—der Vater des *Dichters.*
Hectoris Andromache—servus *Ciceronis*—templa *deorum.*
ἡ νίκη τῶν Ἀθηναίων—ἡ δεινότης Περικλέους.
Used predicatively:
This house was *Shakespeare's* (= belonged to Shakespeare).—
Shakespeare is *ours* (gen. formed from the possessive adj. *our*).

given it is to be understood that English uses a phrase formed with 'of' or some other preposition.

Die schöne Müllerin ist *mein* (= *meiner*, gen.).
Omnia quae *mulieris* fuerunt *viri* fiunt.
Ἕκτορος ἥδε γυνή (Il. vi. 460).

(ii) **Genitives of connexion,** denoting 'connected with' in a wide sense of the term:

Shakespeare's works [life, marriage, death, portrait]—*everybody's* [*nobody's*] business—a *camel's* shadow—the *sun's* rays—the *earth's* crust—New *Year's* eve—*to-day's* news—the *war's* delays—for *friendship's* sake—at *death's* door—at *one's fingers'* ends.
Goethes Briefe—eine Bemerkung *Schillers*—*jedermanns* Geschäft—der Schatten der *Bäume*—des *Jahres* Erzeugniss—die Verzögerungen des *Krieges.*
expeditio [commentarii] *Caesaris*—radii *solis*—simulacra *deorum*—*amicitiae* causa—*belli* vicissitudines [morae].
ἡ εὔνοια τοῦ Σωκράτους—ἀνδριὰς τοῦ Φειδίου—περὶ ὄνου σκιᾶς μάχεσθαι—ἐν πτώσει κύβων.

Used predicatively:

It is *ours* to do and to dare.
Du bist des *Todes* [des *Teufels*].
Imperatoris est consilio non minus quam gladio vincere.
Οὐ τῶν νικώντων ἐστὶ τὰ ὅπλα παραδιδόναι.

(iii) **Genitives of respect,** denoting 'in respect of', 'in point of', are a special kind of genitive of connexion:

Er wird seines *Gutes* nimmer froh (Luther, and not quite obsolete).—Er ist seines *Leibes* und *Lebens* nicht sicher.
sanus *mentis* aut *animi* (Plautus, Trin. 454)—felix *cerebri*—integer *vitae sceleris*que purus—securus *futuri*—Me *consili* sui (= de consilio suo) certiorem fecit.
αὐθάδης φρενῶν—μακάριος τῆς τύχης [τοῦ δέρματος]—τυφλὸς τοῦ μέλλοντος—κωφὸς τοῦ νουθετοῦντος.

Depending on verbs of *accusing, condemning, acquitting* (genitive of the charge):

Man klagt ihn des *Hochverrats* an.—Er wurde des *Verbrechens* überführt [entlassen].
Accusatus [Damnatus, Absolutus] est *proditionis.*
Αἰτιῶνται [Αἱροῦσιν] αὐτὸν κλοπῆς.

(iv) **Objective genitives**, denoting the object of an activity implied in the governing word (noun, adjective, or verb), are a special kind of genitive of connexion:

Duncan's murderer (= the man who murdered Duncan)— *Lear's* protector—the *boys'* counsellor [teacher]—*Sylvia's* lovers [admirers]—The *battle's* loss may profit those who lose (Shelley).

der Mörder des *Königs*—die Verwaltung des *Vermögens*— *Vaterlands*liebe (= Liebe zum Vaterlande).

interfectores *Caesaris*—amor *sui*—metus *mortis*—cupiditas *divitiarum*—memoria *rerum* praeteritarum.

φονεὺς ἑαυτοῦ — ἔρως τῆς ἀρετῆς — ἐπιθυμία τῆς σοφίας—μνήμη τοῦ ἔμπροσθεν χρόνου.

Depending on particular adjectives and verbs:

der *Sache* gewahr—des *Krieges* kundig—des *Lichts* begierig— *Geldes* [*Trostes*] bedürftig—der *Sache* eingedenk—Wir gedenken der *Toten*.—Vergissmeinnicht ('forget-me-not'; *mein* = *meiner*, gen.).—Ich bedürfe deiner *Liebe*.

gnarus [ignarus] *loci*—peritus [imperitus] *belli*—cupidus *sapientiae*—egens *opis*—memor [immemor] *rerum* praeteritarum—*Vivorum* memini neque obliviscor *mortuorum*.

ἐπιστήμων τέχνης—ἔμπειρος [ἄπειρος] τοῦ πολέμου— ἐπιθυμητικὸς [πρόθυμος] τῆς σοφίας—πολλῶν ἐνδεής— μνήμων τοῦ ἔμπροσθεν χρόνου—Μέμνησο τῆς κοινῆς τύχης.—Ἰθάκης οὐκ ἐπιλήσεται.—Ὁ μηδὲν ἀδικῶν οὐδ- ενὸς δεῖται νόμου.

(v) **Descriptive genitives:**

(*a*) Of measurement; joined with nouns that imply extension in time or space:

a *year's* delay—a *month's* grace [notice]—a *day's* march—a nine *days'* wonder—a *night's* rest—a *moment's* hesitation—a *hair's* breadth—at *arm's* length—at a few *miles'* distance—within a *stone's* throw.

um keines *Haares* Breite (rare in modern German).

spatium decem *dierum*—murus centum *pedum*—intra *teli* iactum.

ὁδὸς τριῶν ἡμερῶν—τεῖχος ἕκατον ποδῶν—μέχρι λίθου βολῆς.

(b) Of quality or characteristic; joined with nouns that denote persons, animals, or sometimes inanimate things:

ein Jüngling edlen *Gefühles* (poetical). Used predicatively: Sei frohen *Mutes* [reinen *Herzens*, guter *Laune*].—Er ist meiner *Ansicht*.—Wir sind desselben *Glaubens*.

vir magni *ingeni*—homo *nihili* ('a man of naught'; cf. 'a thing of naught', Shakesp. Mid. Night's Dream iv. 2. 14).—belua multorum *capitum*—saxum magni *ponderis*. Used predicatively: res incerti *exitus* est.

τόλμης πρόσωπον ('a front of daring', Soph. O.T. 533)—χιόνος πτέρυξ (Ant. 114): rare and poetical, except when used predicatively, as in τῆς αὐτῆς γνώμης εἰμί 'I am of the same opinion'.

(vi) Genitives of estimated value:

Er ist deiner *Liebe* nicht wert.—Er würdigt mich seiner *Freundschaft*.

Latin and Greek genitives of estimated value are closely related in meaning to descriptive genitives (v. b) used predicatively:

Nihili est (lit. 'It is of naught' = It is worth nothing).—Hanc domum *magni* [*pluris, plurimi*] aestimo [habeo, duco]. Οὐδενὸς [Πολλοῦ, Πλείονος, Πλείστου] ἄξιός ἐστιν.—Ὑμᾶς οὐδενὸς λόγου ἀξιῶ [τιμῶ].

(vii) Genitives of purchase price or penalty:

Hortos *tanti* emit *quanti* voluit.—*Quanti* vendidit?—*Capitis* damnatus est.
Πόσου διδάσκει;—Πέντε μνῶν.

These genitives were probably developed out of genitives of estimated value (vi): for the case used to express purchase price in the parent language was the sociative-instrumental: cf. the Latin usage, 56. v.

(viii) **Genitives of material,** denoting that of which a thing is made or consists or is full:

eine Menge *Fliegen*—ein Haufen *Leute*—ein Schwarm *Bienen*— eine Heerde *Kühe.* These plurals are felt as genitives, though the genitive inflexion has been lost.

montes *auri*—flumina *lactis*—copia *frumenti*—multitudo *hominum.*

στέφανος ἴων καὶ ῥόδων—ἐσμὸς μελισσῶν [γυναικῶν, νόσων, λόγων]—πλῆθος νεῶν—παράδεισος παντοίων δένδρων.

Depending on particular adjectives and verbs:

amnis plenus [inanis] *aquae* [*piscium*]—carcer completus *mercatorum*—Convivium *vicinorum* compleo (Cicero, de Sen. 46).

Instead of the genitive a sociative-instrumental ablative is often used in Latin: cf. § 56. iv.

ποταμὸς πλήρης [πλέως, κενὸς] ὕδατος [ἰχθύων]—Ναῦς πληροῦται ἀνδρῶν.—Νεκρῶν πληθύει πέδον.

(ix) **Appositive genitives,** used like a noun in apposition:

England's green and pleasant land (Blake; poetical). die Tugenden der *Gerechtigkeit* und des *Grossmuts.* frustum *pueri* ('a bit of a boy')—deliciae *pueri* ('a beauty of a boy')—flagitium *hominis* ('a monstrosity of a fellow'). μέγα χρῆμα συός ('a monster of a boar', 'a regular brute of a boar').

These genitives seem to have been developed out of genitives of material: 'a treasure of a wife' = a treasure consisting in a wife; 'a curiosity of a man' = a curious object consisting in a man, etc. But the meaning is rather 'a wife who is a treasure', 'a man who is a curious object', etc.

(x) **Partitive genitives,** denoting a divided whole, i.e. the whole of which a part is named or sometimes left unnamed[1]:

ein Teil des *Volks*—viele [wenige] der *Einwohner*—unser einer—*ihrer* hundert—*Abends* 'in the course of the evening'.

---

[1] This is probably one of the earliest uses of the Indo-European genitive.

pars *populi*—tantum [quantum] *auri*—multi [pauci] *Gallorum*—
duo *nostrum*—tria milia *militum*—sapientissimus *omnium*—
nox (= noctis) 'by night', e.g. Plautus, Asin. 597; cf. *de nocte*.
πολλοὶ [ὀλίγοι, ὁ κάλλιστος, etc.] τῶν Τρώων—νυκτός
'by night', e.g. Homer, Od. xiii. 278.

Used predicatively:

Fies nobilium tu quoque *fontium*.—Scribe tui *gregis* hunc.
Ἤθελε τῶν μενόντων εἶναι.

Depending on particular adjectives, adverbs and verbs:

des *Bundes* teilhaftig—woher des *Weges*?—spät *Abends*—genug
des *Streites*—Sorgsam brachte die Mutter des klaren herrlichen
Weines (Goethe).

particeps *praemi*—expers *consili*—ubi *terrarum*?—sero *diei*—
satis *litium*—aliquem sui *consili* participare (Plautus, Cist. 165).
μέτοχος [ἄμοιρος] τιμῆς—κοινωνὸς σοφίας—ποῖ γῆς;—
εἴ που τῆς χώρας—ὀψὲ τῆς ἡμέρας—ἅλις λόγων—μετέ-
χειν [μεταλαγχάνειν] ἀθανασίας—τυγχάνειν ἐπαίνου—
ἅπτεσθαι [γενέσθαι, πάσασθαι] σίτου—πιεῖν οἴνου.

II. THE GENITIVE IMPROPER

§ 53. *Ablatival Genitives* (§ 14) without a preposition are found
only in Greek[1]. They correspond to ablatives proper in Latin
(§ 55), and may be classified as genitives of (i) separation, (ii) cause,
conceived as that *from* which a result springs, (iii) standard of comparison, i.e. the point of view *from* which a thing is judged as
greater or less *than* or different *from* something else.

USES OF THE ABLATIVE WITHOUT
A PREPOSITION

§ 54. The ablative has survived as a distinct case in only one of
our six languages, viz. Latin[1]. But owing to the process of case-
amalgamation the Latin ablative has the meanings not only of
the ablative proper but also of two other cases of the parent
language (§ 14).

[1] For this reason it is unnecessary to treat these usages in detail here;
but the parallelisms of Greek and Latin to which attention is called in
§§ 53–57 are very noticeable, and important as verifying the hypothesis
of case-amalgamation. For they could hardly be explained otherwise.

§ 55. I. *Ablatives Proper* without a preposition correspond in Latin to ablatival genitives in Greek (§ 53), and may be classified as ablatives of (i) separation, (ii) cause, conceived as that *from* which a result springs, (iii) standard of comparison.

§ 56. II. *Sociative-Instrumental Ablatives* without a preposition correspond in Latin to sociative-instrumental datives in Greek (§ 46), and may be classified as ablatives of (i) association, (ii) attendant circumstances, (iii) accompanying characteristics or qualities, (iv) instrument and means, (v) purchase price, conceived as the means by which a bargain is made, (vi) cause, conceived as that *by* which a result is brought about, (vii) measure of difference, (viii) respect—a usage which is also related to that of the locatival ablative.

§ 57. III. *Locatival Ablatives* without a preposition correspond in Latin to locatival datives in Greek (§ 47), and may be classified as ablatives of (i) place where, (ii) time when.

ABSOLUTE CONSTRUCTIONS

§ 58. The term 'absolute' as applied to these constructions signifies 'having a loosened connexion with the rest of the sentence'. All the languages of our family have 'absolute' constructions; but the fact that the *case* in which they stand differs greatly in the different languages proves that these constructions were developed independently in the several languages, and not derived directly from the parent language. The several languages reached synonymous constructions by different routes. What happened was that a noun or pronoun which originally stood in a particular relation to the verb of the sentence broke away from this relation, and entered into close relation with a predicative participle so as to form with it a new syntactical group, equivalent in meaning to a subordinate clause. The process was analogous to that by which the accusative with infinitive construction was developed (§ 27).

§ 59. The case of the absolute construction in the early Germanic languages (including Anglo-Saxon) was for the most part the dative[1]: e.g. (in Anglo-Saxon) *him gyt sprecendum* literally 'him yet speaking', *gebygedum cneowum* literally 'knees bent'; but in modern English the nominative has been substituted, no doubt because the noun or pronoun was felt to stand in the relation of subject to the predicative participle: *We sitting*, the cock crew loud (Tennyson).—*She failing* in her promise, I have been diverting my chagrin (Sheridan).—*God willing*, we shall prevail. —*Weather permitting*, we shall sail to-morrow.—*This done*, he retired.—*All said and done*, I do not repent.—*Given this*, peace follows as a matter of course (Nicholas Murray Butler).

§ 60. In modern German the case used in this construction is generally the accusative, but sometimes the genitive[2]: *keinen ausgenommen* 'not one excepted'—*eingeschlossen Macherlohn* 'cost of manufacture included'—*kaum geredet das Wort* 'the word scarcely spoken'—*den Fall gesetzt*—*die Hände* zum Zeus *erhoben* (Schiller)—*das Auge* von Weinen *getrübet* (Schiller). The genitive is found in expressions like the following: *eilenden Schrittes—verhängten Zügels—gesenkten [erhobenen] Hauptes—leuchtenden Auges—unverrichteter Sache.*

§ 61. In Latin the case ordinarily used was the ablative, which may be regarded in some instances as an ablative proper (§ 55. ii), in others as a locatival ablative (§ 57. ii), in others as a sociative-instrumental ablative (§ 56. ii, iii, vi). In most instances the last named suits the context, so that the ablative absolute group may generally be translated by a phrase formed with the preposition 'with': *magna comitante caterva* 'with a great troop accompanying him' (Virgil, Aen. ii. 40), *paucis defendentibus* 'with few defending

---

[1] Grimm (Deutsche Grammatik IV, pp. 893–919) showed that the construction is not due to foreign influence. Brugmann (K. V. Gram. § 815) regarded the absolute dative in Gothic as developed out of a dative proper: e.g. *sitandin imma* 'to him sitting', in Ulfilas' translation of καθημένου αὐτοῦ (Matth. xxvii. 19). Sweet, however, treated the absolute dative in Anglo-Saxon as sociative: e.g. *him sprecendum* 'with him speaking', *gewunnenum sige* 'with victory won' (Anglo-Saxon Primer, p. 41).

[2] The precise origin of these uses is somewhat obscure. Grimm (*op. cit.* pp. 906 f.) explained the accusative by the ellipse of the participle *habend* 'having'; this, however, involves a non-absolute origin of the construction.

it', *omnibus rebus comparatis* 'with everything made ready'. Such groups, however, easily assume various shades of meaning according to the context in which they stand: *signo dato*, lit. 'with the signal given' = on (or owing to) the giving of the signal; *volente deo*, lit. 'with the god willing' = if (or because) the god is willing: cf. *cum dis volentibus* (Plautus, Persa 332)[1].

§ 62. In French the case used is the accusative: *la partie finie* 'the game finished'—*la main levée* 'the hand raised'—*elle régnant* = illa regnante—Ainsi se passèrent cette journée et les suivantes, *madame de Couaën ne me faisant* aucune mention des lettres reçues (Sainte Beuve, Volupté xv. 220). This French use may perhaps be explained as due to the encroachment of the accusative upon the sphere of other cases, which is a marked feature in the development of various constructions in many languages. That the case in French is historically an accusative and not a nominative is proved by Old French and Provençal, where a distinct accusative form of the participle is employed.

§ 63. In Spanish the case used is the nominative, as in modern English: *Trabajando yo* ('I working'), vino un negrito.—*Pasado el verano* ('the summer past'), invernaron en Cuenca.—*Quitada la causa* ('the cause having been removed'), se quita el pecado (Don Quixote).—*Dios mediante* 'God helping'—*no obstante eso* 'this not withstanding' (= notwithstanding this).

§ 64. In Greek the absolute case is ordinarily the genitive, which in some instances may be regarded as a genitive proper, e.g. σέθεν ἐγὼ οὐκ ἀλεγίζω χωομένης 'I care not for thee angered', hence 'thou being angered, I care not' (Iliad viii. 477 f.), but more often as an ablatival genitive (§ 53. ii), e.g. Σαρπήδοντι δ' ἄχος γένετο Γλαύκου ἀπιόντος 'owing to the departure of Glaucos' (Iliad xii. 392). Out of such constructions sprang that use of the genitive absolute in which the case cannot be

---

[1] In late Latin a nominative absolute and an accusative absolute are sometimes found: Cui, *coniunx moriens*, non fuit alter amor (quoted by Engström, Carmina Latina Epigraphica, 358. 8); *structores C. Manium et G. Aemilium* (Dessau, Inscriptiones Latinae Selectae, Vol. III, Part ii, No. 9395): cf. Lofstedt, Peregr. Aetheriae, pp. 158 ff.

regarded as depending on the verb at all, e.g. οὔ τις ἐμεῦ ζῶντος σοι βαρείας χεῖρας ἐποίσει (Iliad i. 88); here ἐμεῦ ζῶντος 'I living' has been fully developed into an equivalent for a subordinate clause ('while I live').

The Greek accusative absolute is far more limited in use, being found chiefly in impersonal expressions like ἐξόν 'it being lawful'—παρόν—δέον, etc., but also in expressions introduced by ὡς or ὥσπερ, e.g. ὡς περιεσομένους ἡμέας (Herod. ix. 42).

CASE-PHRASES

§ 65. There was nothing in the nature of things to limit the number of the cases in the parent language of the Indo-European family to eight: in some languages of other families (e.g. Finnish) there are many more than eight cases. And in Indo-European the case-system was supplemented from prehistoric times by another system, which may be called the case-phrase system. By a 'case-phrase' is meant a phrase consisting of a preposition + an oblique case, the two words being together analogous in function to an oblique case without a preposition[1].

§ 66. Case-phrases served several purposes:

(i) They provided the means of expressing relations which could not be expressed at all by any bare case. Thus case-phrases came into being as an essential supplement to cases, and they exist in all the languages of our family, though they are not generally described by the term 'case-phrase'. For example, the relations of 'before' and 'after', 'above' and 'below' were not

---

[1] The term 'case-phrase' was a creation of the British Joint Committee on Terminology (Report, p. 27). As there defined, the term had the wide meaning in which it is used in the present volume. It has been misinterpreted, however, by Prof. Allen Mawer in The Problem of Grammar, p. 14. Some case-phrases are identical in meaning with one or another of the oblique cases without a preposition and may therefore be called 'genitive-phrases', e.g. the wit of man = man's wit, 'dative-phrases', e.g. give it to me = give it me, 'accusative-phrases', e.g. ad urbem ire = Romam ire, or 'ablative-phrases', e.g. summa cum cura scribere = summa cura scribere. But most case-phrases express meanings which cannot be expressed by any bare case, and are therefore not *equivalent* to any case.

expressed by any of the eight cases of the parent language; they could be expressed only with the help of prepositions.

(ii) They gave greater precision to the meanings suggested (though only imperfectly expressed) by the bare cases; the need for such differentiation became increasingly necessary after the meanings of the cases had been widened through the process of case-amalgamation. Thus in Greek the ablatival genitive might be distinguished from the genitive proper by adding such prepositions as ἀπό, ἐκ; and the sociative dative from the dative proper by adding σύν: in Latin the addition of *cum* distinguished the sociative ablative from other ablatives: and so forth.

(iii) They lent variety and picturesqueness to speech by providing alternative methods of expressing meanings which were already expressed by bare cases. For example, 'place whither' was expressible by a bare accusative in Greek and Latin (§ 28); but another means of expressing this meaning lay to hand and gradually gained ground, viz. the accusative preceded by a preposition meaning 'towards': εἰς τὴν πόλιν, ad [*in*] *urbem*. The bare accusative fell out of use in this sense in Attic Greek, and to a great extent in Latin also, though it was retained for the names of towns and small islands and a few other words (*rus, domum, foras*), and in poets occasionally for other nouns (e.g. *Italiam* venit; devenere *locos*; *speluncam* eandem devenient: Virgil, Aen. i. 2, 365; iv. 124). 'Place whence'—expressible by the bare genitive in Greek (§ 53. i) and by the bare ablative in Latin (§ 55. i)—came to be usually expressed by such case-phrases as ἐκ (or ἀπὸ) τῆς πόλεως, *ex* (or *ab*) *urbe*. It was probably the use of prepositions in expressions of 'place where' that led to the ultimate extinction or absorption of the old locative case, except in a few isolated survivals (§ 16). Illustrations of this development of case-phrases at the expense of bare cases might be multiplied almost indefinitely: it has been going on in all Indo-European languages from very early times[1].

---

[1] See Wackernagel, Vorlesungen über Syntax, Zweite Reihe (1924), pp. 216 ff. Among his instances he quotes Herodotus iii. 16 (end) αἱ ἐκ τοῦ Ἀμάσιος ἐντολαί and Thucydides viii. 21. 1 ἡ ὑπὸ τοῦ δήμου ἐπανάστασις, in which the meanings of the case-phrases might have been sufficiently (though not quite so explicitly) expressed by the bare genitive.

§ 67. Prepositions have been created out of adverbs. In sentences like νύμφη δ' ἐτίθει πάρα πᾶσαν ἐδωδήν 'the nymph placed all kinds of food hard by' (Homer, Od. v. 196), ἐκ δ' εὐνὰς ἔβαλον, κατὰ δὲ πρυμνήσι' ἔδησαν 'and out they cast the mooring-stones, and down they fastened the hawsers' (Il. i. 436), *i prae* 'go ahead' (Plautus and Terence, e.g. Pseud. 170, Andr. 171), the words παρά, ἐκ, κατά, *prae* are clearly adverbs; but such adverbs came to be used in juxtaposition to a case of a noun or pronoun, in such a way as to form a single composite expression having adverbial meaning. Out of this parathetic use of adverbs a new part of speech, called by the inadequate name of 'preposition', was created: for example, ἐκ δ' ἄγαγε κλισίης Βρισηΐδα καλλιπάρῃον 'out (adverb) he led the fair Briseis from-the-hut' (ablatival genitive, Il. i. 346) developed into ἐκ κλισίης ἄγαγε or ἐκ τῆς κλισίης ἤγαγε 'from (preposition) the hut he led', etc.; and Σκύρῳ ἔνι τρέφεται φίλος υἱός 'at-Skyros (locative) within (adv.) is nurtured my dear son' (Il. xix. 326) developed into ἐν (prep.) Σκύρῳ τρέφεται, etc.

§ 68. The association of particular cases with particular prepositions was obviously determined in the first instance by affinities of meaning. There is no difficulty in seeing why ἀπό 'from' took an ablatival genitive, or why ἐν 'in' took a locatival dative; similarly prepositions meaning 'into' or 'towards' naturally took an accusative denoting direction (§ 28). In some instances the main burden of expressing the meaning was thrown upon the case; e.g. παρὰ τὸν βασιλέα 'to the king', παρὰ τῷ βασιλεῖ 'by the side of the king', παρὰ τοῦ βασιλέως 'from the king'. But in some case-phrases it is difficult to see any special propriety in the case. It is, indeed, often quite uncertain how a particular preposition came to 'rejoice in' a particular case—to use the picturesque metaphor employed by old-fashioned grammarians. One fact of cardinal importance must be borne in mind—the

And he calls attention to the encroachment of διά and περί with the genitive, ἐν with the dative, and εἰς with the accusative in Attic Greek, as compared with Homeric expressions in which no preposition was used: e.g. διέπρησσον πεδίοιο ('over the plain'); τῆς ('for her') ἀχέων; αἰθέρι ('in the aether') ναίων; ἱκώμεθα δώματα ('to the home') πατρός.

gradual encroachment of the accusative on the domain of other cases. The Greek ἀνά, which in Homer is used with all the three oblique cases, is hardly used with any other case than the accusative in Attic; and there was a general tendency to eliminate the dative with ἀμφί, μετά and περί[1]. In modern Greek all prepositions take the accusative usually[2]. In Latin of all periods the great mass of prepositions take only the accusative: there may have been a movement from multiplicity towards uniformity within Latin itself. In late Latin the encroachment of the accusative went much further: *cum* is found with the accusative in two inscriptions of so early a date as the first century A.D.[3], and in later centuries such expressions as *cum coniugem suam, ab aedem, pro salutem* become common.

§ 69. In French, Spanish, and English the case of words depending on prepositions can be determined only by historical and analogical considerations. A careful examination of the history of the forms in the chief Romance languages led Diez to the conclusion that the case of nouns depending on prepositions must be regarded as the accusative in this group of languages[4]. And the 'tonic' forms of personal pronouns, when used in dependence on prepositions, function as accusatives. In Anglo-Saxon two cases were chiefly used in dependence on prepositions: some prepositions took the accusative, some a dative (mostly a dative improper, with sociative or ablatival or locatival meaning), but the majority admitted either the dative or the accusative, especially in late Anglo-Saxon. This alternative was sometimes significant of a distinction of meaning—the dative being used with verbs denoting rest and the accusative with verbs denoting

---

[1] The accusative with ἀμφί and περί 'around', 'about', μετά 'after', and διά 'through' may, no doubt, have been developed out of adverbial accusatives (§ 28). So too the accusative with *circum, post, per*. But the connexion of meaning is not very close.

[2] This fact shows how little we can expect to find any *propriety* in the cases used with prepositions in modern languages.

[3] Saturninus *cum discentes* (Dessau, *op. cit.* No. 6419 *e*); Tyrannus *cum sodales* (*ibid.* No. 6418 *c*).

[4] Diez, Grammatik der romanischen Sprachen, Book IV (Syntax), p. 153; cf. Book II (Wortbiegungslehre), pp. 5 ff.

motion, as in modern German (§ 15); in such instances the dative was locatival and the accusative denoted direction. But in many instances the two cases were used promiscuously, without any clear distinction of meaning[1]; here the accusative was not an accusative proper, i.e. it was out of touch with the meanings which the accusative had in the parent language and continued to have, when used without a preposition, in the daughter languages (§§ 23–28). The accusative was in fact an intruder, and its use was due to the tendency of that case to encroach on the domain of other cases, of which we have had many illustrations. In Middle English, when the distinctions of form between the two cases were levelled by phonetic change, it is of course impossible to say whether it is the dative or the accusative that survives in dependence on those prepositions which took either of these cases without distinction of meaning in Anglo-Saxon. In modern English it may fairly be said that all sense of a distinction between the two cases in dependence on prepositions has been blotted out[2].

§ 70. *Survey of results.* The close parallelism of usage between the modern and the ancient languages of our family in this department of syntax has now, I hope, been sufficiently demonstrated (§§ 20–69). Such differences as exist are diversities within a unity, and none of them involve any new principle of structure. The development of case-phrases at the expense of cases is not a new feature in modern languages; and it is for the most part limited to two of the cases—the dative and the genitive. It is, therefore, a misrepresentation of the facts to set up an antithesis of 'modern languages' on the one hand and 'ancient languages' on the other, as representing two distinct

---

[1] See Bosworth-Toller's Anglo-Saxon Dictionary under *and* (= 'with' or 'against'), *æfter, æt, for, fore, beforan, in, mid* (= 'with'), *ofer, on, oþ* (= 'to', 'until'), *tō, under, wiþ, wiþūtan.*

[2] In these circumstances the British Terminology Committee, in view of the need of giving some simple rule for the teaching of English, appealed to the analogy of Latin, French, and modern Greek and recommended that *if the case depending on a preposition in English be named* it be called the accusative; and the American Committee classified the case used with prepositions under the head of the accusative.

types of speech, severed from one another by a great gulf. Let not man presume to tear asunder what Nature has joined together.

An evolution there has no doubt been; but no revolution. The modern is linked to the ancient by an unbroken line of descent. The dative-phrases of French and Spanish are simply developments of dative-phrases found in all periods of Latin, in which the preposition *ad* had lost a great part of its local meaning: *dare ad* is found even in Plautus and Terence (Epid. 38, Phorm. 653), *scribere ad, fari ad, clamare ad, inquit ad* in Lucilius (598), Cicero (Timaeus 40), Catullus (67. 14, cf. 61. 219), Horace (Sat. ii. 6. 90). In post-classical Latin such expressions became commoner: e.g. *alter ad alterum dicebat* (Tertullian). In Merovingian Latin they were largely developed and extended in use, for example in the History of the Franks by Gregory of Tours: in a sixth-century inscription we read *hic requiescunt membra ad duos fratres* ('belonging to two brothers'). The development of these dative-phrases is an interesting chapter of historical grammar which cannot be set forth in detail here; so too the development of the genitive-phrases in French and Spanish—all derived from Latin *de*-phrases, equivalent to partitive genitives, such as *dimidium de praeda* (Plautus), *pars de istius impudentia* (Cicero), *alter de his duobus* (Caesar), *unus de auxiliaribus* (Livy), *Epicuri de grege porcus* (Horace), *hoc de te* (Virgil, Aen. ix. 491, 'this bit of thyself', referring to the decapitated head of Euryalus). In Vitruvius the partitive genitive is almost entirely superseded by *de* or *ex* with the ablative. In late Latin *de* is the sole survivor of the three prepositions which had competed with one another for existence in partitive expressions (*ab, ex, de*), and the *de*-phrases have almost entirely dispossessed the old partitive genitive. Moreover they have begun to be used in other than partitive expressions—as equivalent to instrumental and causal ablatives and to ablatives of comparison. Here we have many of the characteristic usages of the modern French *de*-phrases anticipated; so that it is difficult to say exactly where Latin ends and French begins.

The use of genitive-phrases in English, as substitutes for Anglo-Saxon genitives, has had a curious history. The earliest instances occur in translations from Latin—*of* being taken as the nearest Anglo-Saxon equivalent of the Latin *de*[1]. The cases used with these prepositions corresponded—the Latin ablative to the Anglo-Saxon ablatival dative. It seems, then, that these genitive-phrases, which are so prominent a feature of modern English usage, began their career as Latinisms. Their wider use after the Norman conquest was no doubt due to the influence of the French *de*-phrases (themselves of Latin origin). Whether English would have developed its *of*-phrases apart from Latin and French influence is doubtful[2].

[1] E.g. *monige of Ongelþeode* for *multi de gente Anglorum* in the translation of Bede's History—about 900 A.D., a period when the partitive genitive was in full use in Anglo-Saxon and no substitute for that expression was needed.

[2] See the O.E.D., Vol. VII, pp. 66–70. I gather from my friend Professor Fiedler that the history of the German *von*-phrases was similar, except that it was French rather than Latin influence that brought them into being. The earliest instances known to him occur in Middle High German.

CHAPTER II

ON MOODS AND TENSES

§ 71. The problems to be faced in connexion with moods and tenses are fundamentally the same as those which have been discussed above in connexion with cases. Here, then, I may confine myself to a brief restatement *mutatis mutandis* of principles already familiar to the reader.

§ 72. The conjugation of a verb, like the declension of a noun, is a classification of forms according to their meanings or uses in sentences—a classification which is functional, not morphological, in principle. The forms collected together under the heading of a mood or a tense are often morphologically heterogeneous, e.g. the aorists ἔπεισα and ἔπιθον, the futures φιλήσω and ἔδομαι, *amabo* and *dicam*, the perfects πέπεικα and πέποιθα, *momordi* and *scripsi*, the pasts *saw* and *loved*, *sah* and *liebte*. The Latin 'subjunctive' includes a number of forms which are morphologically optatives, e.g. *sim, sis, sit* (Old Latin *siem, sies, siet* = εἴην, εἴης, εἴη). Nor are the mood and tense forms necessarily distinctive : φιλήσω may be either a future indicative or an aorist subjunctive, *dicam* a future indicative or a present subjunctive, *fuerit* a future perfect indicative or a perfect subjunctive, *vertit* a present or a perfect indicative, *speak* an indicative or an imperative or a subjunctive, *loved* and *liebte* past indicatives or past subjunctives. For a functional classification necessarily brings together in one category forms which from a morphological point of view are heterogeneous, and dissociates forms which are morphologically homogeneous.

§ 73. Aristotle called both moods and tenses πτώσεις of the verb, i.e. verbal cases, and the term πτῶσις ῥηματική is used by Dionysius of Halicarnassus (towards the close of the first century B.C.) in his book on Literary Composition, ch. vi, side by side with another term, ἔγκλισις 'inclination', the precise origin of which is unknown. Its earliest occurrence is in the grammar of Dionysius Thrax of Alexandria, who wrote towards the close of the second century B.C. There the moods are called ἐγκλίσεις and are classified as (i) 'indicating' or 'defining'— ἔγκλισις ἀποφαντική or ὁριστική, (ii) 'commanding', 'imperative'—ἔγκλισις προστακτική, (iii) 'wishing', 'optative'—ἔγκλισις εὐκτική, (iv) 'subordinating'—ἔγκλισις ὑποτακτική. An attempt is here made to name the moods according to certain prominent aspects of the verbal activity denoted by the verbal forms. But the term ὑποτακτική merely registers the fact that the mood is found in subordinate clauses. The Romans translated ὑποτακτική by *subiunctivus* 'subjunctive' or 'subjoining', and thus perpetuated the use of a term which was not merely of a different order from the terms 'indicative', 'imperative', and 'optative', but was positively misleading[1]. Who was responsible for the creation of this unfortunate term we do not know. What a pity that no one thought of calling the mood ἐπιτακτική—a term which would have been translatable by the Latin *iniunctivus*, 'injunctive', i.e. 'enjoining'. This name would have been really descriptive of one at least of the fundamental meanings of the mood—that which is akin to the meaning of the imperative.

§74. The term ἔγκλισις, literally 'inclination', may have originally suggested nothing more than the term πτῶσις, i.e. 'deflection'. But Apollonius Dyscolus, an Alexandrian grammarian of the second century A.D., regarded the moods as expressing ψυχικαὶ διαθέσεις 'attitudes of mind' (*inclinationes animi*). And the Latin term *modus* may have originated in some such conception: Quintilian (Instit. Orat. i. 5. 41) suggests as alternatives the terms *status* and *qualitas*. The English 'mood' as a technical term of grammar is a curious blend of the Latin *modus* and the Germanic *mut* 'state of mind or feeling'.

§75. The Greek names for the tenses (χρόνοι) can be traced

---

[1] Some Roman grammarians called the mood *coniunctivus*, and explained this term as signifying that the mood never stood alone, but always *joined to itself* another mood (the indicative). This term, then, was based on the same misconception as the term *subiunctivus*: they both ignored the non-dependent uses of the mood.

to an earlier source. They were the creations of Stoic grammarians, who herein showed their remarkable scientific insight. These grammarians had seized on the fundamentally important point that tenses may denote something more than simple time relations : they may mark an activity not merely as past, present, or future, but also as in progress or as completed, i.e. they may indicate the stage of development as well as the time of the activity. The tenses of progressive action were described by the Stoics as 'extending alongside' (παρατατικοί) or as 'not completed' (ἀτελεῖς), those of completed action as 'having reached their end' (συντελικοί or sometimes τέλειοι). All the tenses that denoted the two aspects of time and stage of action they called 'definite' (ὡρισμένοι), as distinct from tenses which did not define the action as either in progress or completed, but marked only its time (past or future). These two tenses they called 'indefinite' (ἀόριστοι). The Stoics, then, conceived of the tenses as indicating time, with or without an indication of other aspects of the activity; and this is the right way of regarding them[1].

§ 76. THE STOIC SCHEME OF TENSES

I. χρόνοι ὡρισμένοι :

1. Action defined as in progress or not completed :

(a) at the time of speaking: παρατατικὸς ἐνεστώς (praesens imperfectum[2]), e.g. γράφω.

(b) at some point of time in the past which the speaker has in mind: παρατατικὸς παρῳχημένος (praeteritum imperfectum[2]), e.g. ἔγραφον.

[1] The aspects other than those of past, present, and future time are called *Aktionsarten* (kinds of activity) by most modern German grammarians; and many more 'kinds of activity' are recognized than the Stoics took account of: see Brugmann-Thumb, Griechische Grammatik, pp. 538 ff., Giles, Manual of Comparative Philology, §§ 543 ff., Moulton, Grammar of New Testament Greek, Vol. I, chap. VI.

[2] This Latin translation of the Stoic term is taken from Priscian, Institutiones Grammaticae, Book VIII. For the other Latin translations inserted in brackets on p. 54 and in §§ 103–116 I am responsible.

2. Action defined as completed:

   (*a*) at the time of speaking: συντελικὸς ἐνεστώς (praesens perfectum), e.g. γέγραφα.

   (*b*) at some point of time in the past which the speaker has in mind: συντελικὸς παρῳχημένος (praeteritum perfectum), e.g. ἐγεγράφη.

II. χρόνοι ἀόριστοι:

   1. Action marked as simply past, i.e. prior to the time of speaking: ἀόριστος παρῳχημένος (praeteritum indefinitum), shortened in practice to ἀόριστος, e.g. ἔγραψα.

   2. Action marked as simply future, i.e. posterior to the time of speaking: ἀόριστος μέλλων (futurum indefinitum), shortened in practice to μέλλων, e.g. γράψω.

Note that the Stoics classified the form ἐγεγράφη correctly (as a Past Perfect, I. 2 *b*)[1]: the omission of the Future Perfect was no doubt due to its rarity in the active voice (τεθνήξω, ἑστήξω).

§ 77. Moods and tenses may be defined as *collections of verb-forms (simple or compound) used, or capable of being used, in indicating particular groups of aspects of the verbal activity in sentences.* The verb-form need not be *distinctive* of the aspect; for form is only one of the agencies whereby distinctions of meaning in moods and tenses, as in cases, are indicated. Let a few examples suffice. The words *cui bono fuerit* in Cicero's second Philippic (35) might mean 'who will be found to have profited thereby?' i.e. *fuerit* might be taken as a future perfect indicative in a non-

---

[1] The Stoic scheme was clumsily recast at a later date in a form which is found in Dionysius Thrax; and it is in this distorted form that it has come down to modern times, and still figures in most Latin grammars of all countries. The great mistake lay in classifying γέγραφα as a tense of *past time*, which involved the further blunder of distinguishing ἐγεγράφη from γέγραφα by the absurd title ὑπερσυντελικός, *plusquamperfectum*, 'more than completed' (shortened from παρεληλυθὼς ὑπερσυντελικός, *praeteritum plusquamperfectum*). The name given to γέγραφα in this scheme was παρακείμενος (shortened from παρεληλυθὼς παρακείμενος, i.e. 'tense of past time lying near to the time of speaking').

dependent question: for the question of Cassius might possibly have been *Cui bono fuerit?* 'To whom will it have been an advantage?' But in this context the words that follow (Quamquam illud *fuit*, ut tu dicebas, omnibus bono..., tibi tamen praecipue) show that *fuerit* is to be taken as a perfect subjunctive in a dependent question: 'the question of Cassius *as to who profited* (or *has profited*) *thereby*'. In this instance it is the context alone that shows the mood and tense of the ambiguous form *fuerit*. In other instances the mood and tense are shown by the order of words or by the phrasing and intonation of the sentence: e.g. *Fuerint* cupidi, *fuerint* irati, *fuerint* pertinaces 'granted that they were...' (perfect subjunctive, Cic. pro Ligario 18); *Liebte* er mich, so würde er sich anders betragen, *Did* he *love* me, he would behave differently (past subjunctives). Sentences containing imperatives are naturally pronounced with a special intonation in all languages; e.g. 'Speak, Lord'. Contrast 'Let me go!' with 'He let me go'. Thus the intonation of the sentence as a whole may direct the attention of the hearer to its modal meaning and enable him, if he is a grammarian, to identify the mood contained in it.

§ 78. The words 'particular *groups* of aspects' in the above definition (§ 77) point to the important fact that each mood and each tense has a certain range of meaning, i.e. embraces a whole group or area of more or less distinct meanings. Moreover these groups or areas of meaning are not sharply demarcated; they overlap one another to a certain extent. Two overlapping moods or tenses may be compared to two intersecting circles: the area enclosed by the intersecting circumferences is not excluded from either circle, but belongs to both of them. Thus a meaning that is expressible by one mood or tense is often alternatively expressible by another. For example, the future indicative may be used to express not only pure futurity but also command or request (as in 'The congregation *will rise* with the choir', 'Tu nihil invita *dices* faciesve Minerva', Horace, Ars poetica 385), or promise (as in 'Cras *donaberis* haedo', Odes iii. 13. 3), or resolve (as in 'Immo ego *ibo*', Terence, Adelphi 604), or obligation (as in 'Quid *fiet*?' 996, 'Quid *faciemus*?' Hec. 668), or mere probability (as in 'Haec *erit* bono genere nata', Plautus, Persa 645)—meanings which are expressible by an imperative or a subjunctive or in other ways.

§ 79. Again, the present indicative is not limited to expressions of present time: it has a certain elasticity of meaning, so that we can say 'I start for Paris to-morrow' in the sense of 'I shall start' or 'I am to start', i.e. I am bound to start. It must always be borne in mind that the present of human experience, and therefore of grammar, is not a point of time without dimensions, separating off two eternities: this is a metaphysical, not a grammatical, conception. The present of grammar is a period of time, having a certain duration: it centres in the moment of speaking, but it extends (if only a little distance) into the past and into the future. When a man says 'I love you', he does not mean that his love is limited to the moment of speaking. This elasticity of the present tense is a characteristic feature of all the languages of our family. In particular this tense is frequently pregnant with an idea of futurity, i.e. it denotes a present obligation or resolve as to the performance of some future act: αὔριον γὰρ ἀποθνήσκομεν 'for to-morrow we *die*' (1 Corinthians xv. 32); *Eo*, domine 'I *go*, sir' (Matthew xxi. 30; cf. *eo* and *non eo* = 'I will go' and 'I won't go' in Plautus, Most. 853, 877, and *circumeo* in Caesar, B.C. iii. 94. 5); *Quiescis?* 'Will you hold your tongue?' (Plautus, Rud. 781). 'You *go* not' means 'You shall not go' in Hamlet iii. 4. 19. Quid *ago*? may mean 'What am I *to do*?' (e.g. Plautus, Persa 666), cf. Quam *prendimus* arcem? 'What stronghold *are* we *to occupy*?' (Virg. Aen. ii. 322). Nil *do* may mean 'I *won't give* a penny' (Terence, Phorm. 669). For similar uses of the tense in Greek see Eur. Androm. 381, Aristoph. Wasps 458, Thuc. vi. 77 (μένομεν). In subordinate clauses of English we get examples like 'Take care that you *are* not *caught*', 'England must see to it that this *does* not *occur* again', where a subjunctive or a phrase with 'shall' might have been used to express the meaning.

§ 80. In other instances the present tense makes a statement that is true of all times; but the time of speaking is always included: Twice two is four, Fortes fortuna adiuvat, 'Oψὲ θεῶν ἀλέουσι μύλοι, ἀλέουσι δὲ λεπτά (in Sextus Empiricus), Gottes Mühlen mahlen langsam, mahlen aber trefflich klein (Friedrich von Logau). And past tenses are often used to denote what has been known to occur again and again in the past, and is therefore likely to recur in the future: Faint heart never won fair lady; Men were deceivers ever. Such proverbial sayings are meant to be true of all times, but they refer in the first instance to the past, which is generalized by the words 'ever', 'never' (= 'at all times', 'at no time'). The tense should not be called 'timeless'.

§ 81. The overlapping of the significations of the several moods and tenses, like that of the cases (§ 7), is due to the way in which human speech has been developed all the world over. It was not made to order, so as to correspond to preconceived categories of thought: it grew. And its growth was determined by practical human needs and natural associations of ideas, but without regard to logical consistency or completeness. It has been well remarked that human speech is not a thrifty housewife; she is extravagant with one hand, and parsimonious with the other[1]. She provides a superfluity of expressions for certain meanings, and leaves others unexpressed. This has not always been understood. The grammarians of the early nineteenth century, such as Gottfried Hermann, who based their syntax upon the metaphysical categories of Wolff and Kant, always assumed that language provided one and only one expression for each of these categories. But it is now seen that this assumption is unhistorical and unpsychological, and leads to many grave errors[2]. Grammarians of the present day go to work in an entirely different way. But it must be added that one grammarian of the twentieth century, Professor Jespersen, occupies a position apart, in that he regards the laws of logic and the notions that are 'common to all mankind' as a norm to which all languages ought to conform, and aims at establishing a new kind of grammar based on such notions. He even sits in judgement on the merits of

---

[1] Kroll, Die wissenschaftliche Syntax im lateinischen Unterricht, p. 9.
[2] Hale, A century of metaphysical syntax (Congress of Arts and Science, Boston, 1906, Vol. III, pp. 191–202).

languages as media for the expression of logical relations, and awards them praise or blame according as their syntax appears to him to be logically justified or not[1].

§ 82. It is obvious from the above considerations that none of the names devised by grammarians in ancient or modern times to denote the moods and the tenses of any language can be entirely adequate. It is necessary for grammatical purposes to name the *forms*; and the names given to them must be *functional* names. But these functional names cannot completely cover all the functions of the forms. The best that can be done is to employ for each language names that are significant of the predominant functions in that language and not incompatible with the names employed in other languages. In languages of the same family the moods and tenses, like the cases, have a large community of meaning, so that it is possible to make the same names serve in the several members of the family to a considerable extent, and where the languages go apart to use names which differ only to the extent of these divergences.

§ 83. The above definition of moods and tenses (§ 77) is in touch with the traditional meaning of these terms; and it is deliberately designed to be in disagreement with views expressed or implied by certain recent writers on English grammar. On the one hand we have a school of grammarians who refuse to accept any verb-form as belonging to a mood or tense unless it has its modal or temporal character stamped on its face; i.e. these writers insist that all the forms belonging to a mood or tense must be *distinctive* of that mood or tense: they make form the only criterion of mood and tense[2].

[1] He describes his Philosophy of Grammar as a "preliminary sketch of a notional comparative grammar", and claims it as a merit of his method that it does not restrict him to languages belonging to the same family: *op. cit.* pp. 345 ff.; cf. his Growth and Structure (1926), pp. 12 f.

[2] For example, Mr S. O. Andrew says "The term subjunctive mood should be reserved for those parts of the verb which are subjunctive in form, e.g. I fear lest he *come*, O that '*twere* possible" (The Problem of Grammar, p. 21). Professor Jespersen offers no definition of the terms mood and tense; and his point of view is not easily definable. He tells us that he speaks of 'mood' only when an attitude of mind is shown in the

ON MOODS AND TENSES 59

§ 84. On the other hand we have the diametrically opposite point of view in writers of the school of Wundt. Professor Deutschbein, for example, defines mood as "an expression of a relation in the consciousness of the speaker of what is thought, wished, willed, or expected to reality or to the possibility of realization".[1] According to this definition there are in any language as many moods as there are attitudes of mind to be expressed. Deutschbein recognizes sixteen such moods in English, expressible by a great variety of forms of speech. For example, 'He is sure to come' is classed under the *expectative mood*, 'I wonder whether he knows' under the *dubitative mood*, 'You must go' under the *intensified voluntative mood*, 'I ought to go' under the *unreal voluntative mood*, 'May I go now?' under the *permissive mood*, 'This may be true' under the *potential mood*, 'He would come (if he were not ill)' under the *unreal cogitative mood*, 'He must have been mad' under the *cogitative of necessity*; and so forth. Perhaps my readers will be astonished at Deutschbein's moderation in limiting his moods to sixteen only[2].

form of the verb (Phil. of Gram. p. 313), and in another passage he says that he makes form "the supreme criterion in grammar" (p. 50). But here he warns his readers that the term 'form' is used by him in a sense peculiar to himself, as including "form-words and word-position". And in a recent article (Englische Studien, 1925–26, Vol. 60, p. 301) he adds intonation (*Ton*) as coming under the head of form. He seems, then, to admit that form, in the ordinary meaning of the term, is *not* the only criterion. It would make his position far clearer if he admitted, as my definition does, that modal and temporal functions may be indicated by agencies other than form. I note, however, that Jespersen takes no account of the most important of all these agencies, viz. the context in which the form stands.

[1] System der neuenglischen Syntax, pp. 113 ff. I see no corresponding definition of 'tense'; but Deutschbein evidently regards tenses from a corresponding point of view.

[2] The attitudes of mind that may find expression in speech are extremely multifarious and difficult to classify, whereas the moods that exist in any language are limited in number, though each of them has a certain range of meaning. Thus the relation of attitudes of mind to moods is a highly complicated question, which may be studied in Professor Brunot's La Pensée et la Langue (1922, pp. 507–573). His term for attitudes of mind is 'Modalités de l'idée', and he points out how the same action may present itself in many different lights to our judgement, our sentiments, and our

§ 85. My definition of 'mood' (§ 77) limits the term to *forms of the verb*. The modern English forms to which the term 'subjunctive' is applied in the following pages (including the systematic exposition of the uses of the mood in §§ 126–144) are forms derived from Anglo-Saxon subjunctives or modelled thereon, and are shown to be subjunctives by the context in which they stand. A small minority of them are also recognizable as subjunctives by being *distinctive* forms, i.e. by differing from the corresponding forms of the indicative mood, e.g. *be* as distinct from *am* or *is*, *were* as distinct from *was*, *have* as distinct from *has*.

Past subjunctives, identical in form with past indicatives (except *were*), live on the lips of every speaker of English at the present day. Their chief use is in *if*-clauses which imply unreality or the non-fulfilment of the condition: e.g. 'If he *loved* me, he would behave differently'. Here the implication of 'loved' is shown by the context, i.e. by the main clause of the sentence ('he *would behave* differently'). The modal meaning of this 'loved' is exactly the same as that of 'were' in 'If he *were* my friend, he would behave differently'; both of them refer to present time and imply the unreality of the supposition. But this meaning is shown in the one sentence by the context only, in the other both by the context and by the form of the verb. I have only to add that a past tense of the English subjunctive is the only form of speech at the disposal of a speaker who wishes to draw a comparison based on an impossible condition by the words 'as if'. A recent book, entitled The philosophy of 'as if'[1], teems with examples: e.g. 'Matter must

will. Moods are only one of the means whereby these modalities find expression. An attempt to correlate modalities and moods has been made by Messrs Grattan and Gurrey in Our Living Language (1925, pp. 232–259), but they have confused matters by their tripartite classification of (*a*) modalities of the sentence, (*b*) modalities of the verb, (*c*) moods. [I may add that their criticism of the Terminology Committee's Report (*ibid.* pp. 310f.) is based on a misunderstanding for which they are solely responsible. There is not a word in the recommendation of the Committee (Report, pp. 33 ff.) to justify the inference that the Committee intended the term 'subjunctive' to be limited to distinctive forms of that mood.]

[1] The philosophy of 'as if' by Professor Vaihinger, translated by C. K. Ogden (Kegan Paul, 1924). The German title of this book is Die Philosophie des Als ob.

be treated *as if it consisted of atoms'*, 'Man must act, and his acts must be judged *as if he were a free agent'*, 'We must do our work *as if no one existed—as if no human being lived or had ever appeared on the earth'*, 'Every evil act must be treated *as if the individual had passed to it straight from a condition of innocence'*. The English 'as if' (or 'as though'), like the German 'als ob', always means 'as *would be* (or *would have been) the case if'* ; and in English the verb of the *if*-clause always stands in the past or past perfect subjunctive, denoting the unreality of the condition. Whether the verb is *shown* to be a subjunctive by its form or not does not matter in the least either in the German original of these sentences or in their English translation. The mood is shown in all instances by the words understood after 'as', viz. 'would be (or would have been) the case' ; and in some instances it is *also* shown by the form of the verb. But the reason why we call these forms subjunctives is not that the term is convenient as a guide to *translating* from English into German or Latin (or *vice versa*), but that the English as well as the corresponding German and Latin forms *are* subjunctives both from an historical and from a semantic point of view[1]. Past subjunctives are also unmistakable in sentences like

[1] Modern English past tenses are morphologically just as much subjunctives as indicatives ; that is to say, they correspond to and are derived from two Anglo-Saxon tenses—a past indicative and a past subjunctive. In Anglo-Saxon these two tenses sometimes differed in form (e.g. Indic. *wæs*, Subj. *wære*; Indic. *band*, Subj. *bunde*), sometimes not (e.g. Indic. and Subj. *hierde*, *lufode*): in modern English the two tenses have come to coincide in form (except *was*, *were*), as a result of phonetic changes. But the meanings of the past indicative and the past subjunctive remain very much what they were in Anglo-Saxon times ; and they are felt to be distinct by the modern Englishman. If there were no such thing as historical grammar in existence, it might be difficult to give a grammatical explanation of this twofold meaning of identical forms ; but as it is, there is no such difficulty. Professor Jespersen, however, who refuses the aid of historical grammar and is debarred by his principles from recognizing any difference of mood in the absence of a difference of form (Phil. of Gram. p. 313), is unable to accept two kinds of past tenses: he has to declare that all modern English past tenses (except *was*, *were*) belong to one and the same grammatical category—that of a moodless 'preterite'; and he goes so far as to assert that this 'preterite' has always the same *function*, whatever its notional value may be. This paradox seems to be inherent

'He *could* if he *would*', 'I *would*n't, even if I *could*', 'You *should*n't', 'You *had* better not'.

Present subjunctives are less common in modern English; but they too are necessary in several constructions, for example in such instances as 'It is essential that this practice *be stopped*' (The Times, Feb. 4, 1926), 'I move that Mr A. *take* the chair'. To substitute the indicative 'is stopped' for 'be stopped' or 'takes' for 'take' would make nonsense of the above sentences. And in sentences like 'It is essential that we *stop* this practice', or 'I recommend that you *write* at once', or 'Thank you for suggesting that I *introduce* these instances', the verb of the subordinate clause is a subjunctive; it is shown to be such by the meaning expressed in the main clause. It is, of course, perfectly true that in some instances we cannot tell whether the verb is a subjunctive or an indicative, e.g. in 'If I *come* to see you, will you welcome me?' For there is nothing in the main clause to show the mood of 'come'. And for that very reason the question to which mood the form belongs is of no importance. But in recognizing subjunctives in English I must not be supposed to be pleading for their use. I agree with Mr H. W. Fowler in regarding some current uses of the present subjunctive as affected and not to be encouraged[1].

§ 86. Subjunctives, then, are far from uncommon in modern English. But those subjunctive forms which have been rendered non-distinctive by the levelling effects of phonetic change are very commonly and quite rightly avoided by English speakers and writers, and replaced by phrases which show the meaning more clearly. This only proves how necessary it is to give unambiguous expression to the subjunctive meanings. Such phrases may be called 'subjunctive-equivalents'. Thus for 'we stop' in the above instance it is more explicit to say 'we should stop'; and the

in Jespersen's system; see p. 56 of the work quoted, where the forms *handed, fixed, showed, left, put, drank, was* are bracketed together as having the preterite function, whether they denote past time, or unreality in present time, or future time, etc. See too his pp. 265 f., where he expounds his doctrine of the 'non-temporal use of tenses' at length. Yet there is no difference between modern English and modern German, except that the latter has a larger number of distinct subjunctive forms than the former.

[1] On subjunctives, in S. P. E. Tract, No. XVIII (1924).

meaning of 'take' in 'that Mr A. take the chair' may be more explicitly (though not better) expressed by saying 'should take'. Other subjunctive-equivalents will be given below (§ 125).

§ 87. Let us take a glance at the history of the subjunctive mood. The parent language had, among other moods, a subjunctive and an optative, differing widely in form but closely akin in meaning. They were, in fact, too nearly synonymous to survive side by side in the long run[1]. In classical Sanskrit (the successor of Vedic) the subjunctive fell into disuse, except in the 1st person, which was incorporated in the imperative. In Greek the two moods co-existed during the classical period and were progressively differentiated in use, so that the optative differs more from the subjunctive in Attic than in Homeric Greek or in the Greek of other dialects[2]. But in Hellenistic Greek the optative is already obsolescent, and in modern Greek it has disappeared altogether, except in one literary survival—the expression μὴ γένοιτο. In Latin the subjunctive forms and the optative forms of the parent language were amalgamated in a single mood, which goes by the name of 'subjunctive' or (in Germany) 'Konjunktiv'. And out of this Latin mood were developed the forms which we know as subjunctives in the descendants of Latin. In the Germanic languages the subjunctive became obsolete, and the optative took over its meanings. For the forms used in the Germanic languages are all historically

[1] See an illuminating article by Bréal, entitled Les commencements du verbe (in the Mémoires de la Société de Linguistique, of the date 1900, Vol. XI, pp. 268 ff.). Bréal held that in the earliest form of Indo-European there were only two moods—a mood of 'commandement' (expressing command, wish, prayer, etc.) and a mood of 'accomplissement' (expressing fact, i.e. the indicative). "L'impératif, le subjonctif, et l'optatif avaient tous trois le même rôle. Une si riche synonymie n'a rien que de conforme à ce que nous savons des anciens âges". The later differentiation of these synonymous forms he described as a kind of "échelle dans le genre impératif" (p. 275). In my Unity of the Latin Subjunctive (John Murray, 1910, written long before I had seen Bréal's article) I tried to show that all the uses of the Latin subjunctive are linked together as expressive of the idea of what *is* (or *was*) *to be done*.

[2] See Dr F. Slotty, Der Gebrauch des Konjunktivs und Optativs in den griechischen Dialekten (1915), I, pp. 114 ff.

optatives; but the name 'subjunctive' is extended to them. The Anglo-Saxon 'subjunctives' spoken of in § 85 belong to this class.

§ 88. Apart from the process of mood simplification, and at a later date, there set in another process, which may be described as the encroachment of one mood upon the functional domain of another mood. For example, at an early (but not the earliest) stage of the Greek language, certain tenses of the indicative (past imperfect and aorist) began to be used with meanings which properly belonged to the optative mood. The reason was that the use of the optative in expressions of past unreality was becoming obsolete, and the need was felt of a form which unequivocally denoted past time. The augmented forms of the indicative were pressed into the service, as the only forms available. In expressing the idea of what *would have happened* in certain imagined circumstances of the past, the addition of the word ἄν or κεν indicated that the action was limited by circumstances or restricted by conditions, and thus helped out the meaning and indeed served as the chief means of conveying it; e.g. ἔγνως ἄν, which replaced the older γνοίης ἄν in the sense 'you would have known'[1]. In expressions of unrealizable wish, the meaning of the speaker was indicated by εἴθε (= *utinam*) or εἰ γάρ: e.g. εἴθ' εἶχον, which may be inferred to have replaced an older εἴθ' ἔχοιμι in the sense 'would that I had had'. In both these cases the use of an indicative in a sense that was wholly alien to the sphere of meaning of the indicative proper was an innovation, whereby the range of meaning of the indicative was extended in a startlingly new direction. The same development is seen in the use of past tenses of the indicative in expressing suppositions that were contrary to past

---

[1] Homeric examples of this use of the optative with reference to past time are seen in Iliad v. 311, where κεν ἀπόλοιτο means 'he would have perished', and xvii. 70, where κε φέροι means 'he would have carried off'. The use of the indicative in such sentences is also Homeric, and indeed commoner in Homer than that of the optative, e.g. v. 679 κε κτάνε = 'he would have killed': where Homer has the past imperfect it always refers to past time, e.g. κε οὐτάζοντο 'they would have wounded' or 'would have been wounding', vii. 273. The Attic use of the past imperfect as distinct from that of the aorist (i.e. as referring to present time) is a still later development.

fact, e.g. εἰ ἦλθον (Homer, Il. vii. 273), εἰ ἀνίστατο (xxiii. 491). Hence the Attic use, e.g. εἰ ἦσθα (Soph. Antig. 755, 'if you had been', here and often = 'if you were'). How peculiar these Greek indicatives are is easily seen if one tries the experiment of translating them literally into Latin: εἴθ' εἶχον, *utinam habebam!*

§ 89. A similar acquired meaning of the indicative is found in the modern French use of the past imperfect and past perfect tenses in expressions of unreality introduced by the conjunction *si*: e.g. *si j'étais là* 'if I were there' or 'Would that I were there!'; *si vous l'aviez voulu* 'if you had willed it' or 'Would that you had willed it!'; *je partirais demain, si je le pouvais* (implying *mais je ne le pourrai pas demain*). This construction is a usurpation, which did not come into existence till the 12th century; and it was probably due to the same cause as produced the peculiar Greek constructions just discussed, i.e. the need of finding some form of speech to express a meaning which was no longer clearly expressed by the only surviving past tense of the subjunctive, viz. the forms in *-asse* and *-isse* (derived from Latin past perfect subjunctives); the forms derived from the Latin past subjunctives in *-ārem, -ērem, -ĕrem, -īrem* had all disappeared in Old French. In Old French and even as late as the 17th century in certain writers we find conditional sentences of the above type expressed without the use of the indicative in the *if*-clause: e.g. *Je partisse demain, se* (= si) *je pusse*; *Je partirois demain, se je pusse*; *Je partirois demain, se je pourrois*[1]. But since the 12th century the use of the past imperfect indicative had been gaining ground.

§ 90. The converse invasion of the subjunctive into the domain of the indicative took place in several Latin constructions. In Early Latin (Plautus) *cum*, whether it meant 'when' or 'because' or 'though', ordinarily took the indicative; and dependent questions as to a matter of fact very often took the indicative. In these and similar constructions the use of the subjunctive did not become established till the Ciceronian period; the change is to be regarded as a stylistic innovation, whereby the range of

[1] Instances from Old French literature are quoted by Darmesteter-Sudre, Grammaire Historique de la langue française, IV, pp. 159–165, and Brunot, La Pensée et la Langue, pp. 891, 895.

meaning expressible by the subjunctive was greatly extended. At a somewhat later period (in Livy and Tacitus) the use of the subjunctive was extended to *ever*-clauses, i.e. clauses introduced by words meaning 'whoever', 'whenever', 'wherever', in which Cicero would have used the indicative. Many of the usages found in subordinate clauses of French and Spanish are to be similarly explained.

§ 91. The following paragraphs are concerned with the developed usages of the moods and tenses and their relations, as actually found in the six languages here under consideration. But occasional references to the parent language will be made where its usages throw light upon the developed usages of the daughter languages. It must be distinctly understood, however, that only the most important and prominent among these developed usages can be discussed within the limits of the present treatise. Moods and tenses are the most difficult part of grammar, offering as they do an almost inexhaustible field for observation and speculation. All that can be attempted here is a bird's-eye view of their outstanding relations. For details and subtleties the reader must consult special treatises on the syntax of the ancient and the modern languages.

§ 92. The following map may be useful as a clue to the order of treatment adopted.

THE INDICATIVE PROPER (in all the six languages, §§ 93–117)	INDICATIVES WITH ACQUIRED MEANINGS (in Greek, French, and Spanish, § 118)
THE IMPERATIVE (in all the six languages, §§ 119–123)	
SUBJUNCTIVES AND OPTATIVES PROPER (in all the six languages, §§ 124–140)	SUBJUNCTIVES AND OPTATIVES WITH ACQUIRED MEANINGS (in all the six languages, §§ 141–145)

I. USES OF THE INDICATIVE PROPER
AND ITS TENSES

§ 93. The indicative proper is the most colourless of the moods, and from this point of view the name 'indicative' (= indicating) is very appropriate to it, just because it means so little. All the moods *indicate* something. And if we ask what particular meaning the indicative indicates, the answer is that it often indicates nothing more than the verbal activity in its barest outlines, without any *arrière-pensée*. A present or past tense of the indicative generally (not always) indicates fact. But a future indicative cannot be said to indicate fact; for futurity is never actual. Nor does any tense of the indicative ordinarily express fact when introduced by a word meaning 'if'.

§ 94. The following sections deal with the tenses of the indicative proper. And here the purpose in hand will be best served by taking the Stoic classification of the Greek tenses as it stands (§ 76), and enquiring how far its categories are adequate to the six languages here under consideration. This will bring out in clear relief the relations of agreement and difference in the tenses of these six languages.

I will use the term 'verbal activity' to cover both an 'act' in the narrower sense of the term and a 'state' or 'condition'.

§ 95. Tenses employed to define the verbal activity as either continuing or habitual at the time of speaking. [PRAESENS IMPERFECTUM: § 76, I. 1 *a*.]

The tenses used in expressing these meanings in the six languages have all the same range of meaning, and are therefore all called by the same name, viz. Present.

Whatever *is, is* right.—I *smell* a rat!—Here he *comes*! —Coming events *cast* their shadows before. Ich *bin* der Geist, der stets *verneint*.—Wie *geht's* ?— Gleich und gleich *gesellt* sich gern. Homo *sum*; humani nihil a me alienum *puto*.—Ut

vales? (How do you do?).—Ad quartam *iaceo*; post hanc *vagor*; *unguor* olivo (Horace, Sat. i. 6. 111–130).
Je *sais* ce que vous *voulez*.—Qui s'*excuse*, s'*accuse*.
Sé lo que *quieres*.—No *fumo*.—Quien *canta*, sus males *espanta* (Don Quixote).
Θεῶν ἐν γούνασι κεῖται.—Ὃν οἱ θεοὶ φιλοῦσιν, ἀποθνῄσκει νέος.

§ 96. English and Spanish have a special continuous form to mark an *act* as going on at the time of speaking: I *am writing* a book; *Estoy escribiendo* uno libro. The simple form of the Present in these languages is chiefly used to mark an *act* as habitual or a *state* as existing at the time of speaking. The choice of the one form or the other depends, therefore, upon whether the verb in itself denotes an act or a state.

§ 97. By an extension of its meaning the Present tense is used with adverbial expressions of time to describe an activity as having been continued up to the time of speaking:

From everlasting Thou *art* God (Dr Watts).
Fünf Jahre *trag'* ich schon den glühenden Hass.
Cupio equidem et iam pridem *cupio* Alexandream visere.
Il y a longtemps que je vous *attends*.
Ando desde esta mañana.—With continuous form (§ 96): Hace mucho tiempo que *estoy esperando* a V.
Κάθημαι 'γὼ πάλαι (Aristoph. Wasps 825).

§ 98. The Present tense is also used in vivid or dramatic descriptions of past events, and is then called 'the Historic Present'. But it is still a genuine Present; for it pictures the past as present to the mind's eye. This usage is so familiar in all our six languages that no examples are necessary. The Historic Present was probably a feature of popular speech in very early times, but no examples of it are found in Homer.

§ 99. Examples of wider uses of the Present tense will be found in §§ 79, 80.

§ 100. Tenses employed to define the verbal activity as either continuing or habitual at some point of time in the past which the speaker has in mind. [PRAETERITUM IMPERFECTUM: § 76, I. 1 *b*.]

Here we have the chief meanings of the Present tense transferred to past time (cf. § 95). The tense used in expressing these meanings is the Past Imperfect in Greek, Latin, French, and Spanish[1]. In English and German a tense is used which has also another use (see § 108), and which is therefore called simply Past[2]. Thus the range of meaning of this tense is wider than that of the Past Imperfect of the other languages; but in the usage treated in this section English and German agree exactly with the other languages.

At that time there *was* great unrest: the red flag still *flew* (= was flying) over the Town Hall.—The ancient Greeks sometimes *buried* (= used to bury) their dead, sometimes *cremated* them.

Zu der Zeit *schrieb* er ('he was writing') an einem neuen Buch.—Er *rauchte* ('used to smoke') während der Arbeit.

Hieme anni post urbem conditam DCCII Iulius Caesar commentarios suos *scribebat* ('was writing').—Commentarios suos hieme plerumque *scribebat* ('used to write').

Il *écrivait* ('was writing') sa lettre lorsque je suis arrivé.—Lorsque j'*étais* ('was') malade, il *venait* ('used to come') me voir tous les jours.

Sabía ('I knew') lo que *querías* ('you wanted').—

[1] The American Committee recommends the term 'Past Descriptive' for this tense.

[2] The term commonly used in Germany to describe this tense of the German verb, viz. 'Imperfectum', is a complete misnomer; see exx. p. 74.

Cada noche *volvían* ('used to return') cargados de presa.

Ὁδὸς πρὸς τὸ χωρίον διὰ γηλόφων ὑψηλῶν ἔφερε ('led'), οἳ καθῆκον ('stretched down') ἀπὸ τοῦ ὄρους, ὑφ' ᾧ ἦν ('was') κώμη.—Τὸ ἐνύπνιον ἐπεκέλευέ ('kept urging') με τοῦτο πράττειν ὅπερ ἔπραττον ('was in the habit of doing').

§ 101. English and Spanish have a special continuous form to mark an *act* as going on at the time referred to: I *was writing*; *Estaba escribiendo*.

§ 102. With adverbial expressions of time the simple form of this tense is used in German, Latin, French, and Spanish (but not in Greek) to describe an activity as having been continued up to some point of time in the past which the speaker has in mind (cf. § 97). Here English generally uses the Past Perfect Continuous (§ 107):

Ich *wartete* ('had been waiting') schon zwei Stunden auf ihn.
Multos iam annos domicilium ibi *habebat*.
Il *demeurait* là depuis dix ans.
Andaba desde las diez.

§ 103. Tenses employed to define the verbal activity as already completed at the time of speaking, or to denote a present state resulting from a preceding activity. [PRAESENS PERFECTUM: § 76, I. 2 *a*.]

The tense used in expressing this meaning is in English the Present Perfect, in Greek either the Present Perfect (when attention was directed to the resultant state) or the Aorist (when attention was directed to the preceding act)[1], in Latin, French, Spanish, and German the Perfect—so called because it has also another use in which the relation of the activity to the

[1] This must have been a very early meaning of the Aorist; for in Vedic, the oldest Indian language of our family, this is almost the only meaning of the tense; and it is very common also in Hellenistic Greek; e.g. St John xx. 2 (ἦραν and ἔθηκαν). For a still commoner use of the Aorist see § 108.

time of speaking recedes into the background of consciousness
(§ 108).

What I *have written* I *have written.*—I *have loved*
(= am in the position of having loved) you all my life.

Ich *habe genossen* das irdische Glück,
Ich *habe gelebt* und *geliebet.*

Vixi, et quem dederat cursum fortuna *peregi.*—Nam
nisi qui ipse *amavit,* aegre amantis ingenium inspicit
(Plautus, Mil. 639; cf. Rud. 1320 f.).
Elle *a vécu,* Myrto, la jeune Tarentine ('she has
lived', i.e. her life is over).—Je me *suis trompé.*
Hemos acabado nuestra lectura.—Me *he equivocado.*
Greek Present Perfects : Εὕρηκα ('I've got it !').—
Ἀκήκοα μὲν τοὔνομα, μνημονεύω δ' οὔ.—Οὐδὲ
τεθνᾶσι θανόντες ('but having died they are not
dead'; Simonides, Anth. Pal. vii. 251).
Greek Aorists: Νῦν μὲν γὰρ Μενέλαος ἐνίκησεν σὺν
Ἀθήνῃ (Il. iii. 439).—Ἔφυγον κακόν, εὗρον ἄμει-
νον (a cry of exultation : 'I have escaped an evil, I
have found a better !').—Ἦλθ', ἦλθε χελιδών ('the
swallow is come').

§ 104. English and Spanish have a special continuous form to
mark an *act* as having been performed up to the time of speaking:
I have been writing; *He estado escribiendo.* This form does not
imply the completion of the act: it may still be going on. Thus
the meaning is the same as that which is expressed by the Present
tense with an adverbial expression of time (§ 97).

§ 105. Some Present Perfects and Aorists (called 'gnomic')
denote what has been known to occur in the past and is likely
to recur in the future (§ 80):

The fool *hath said* in his heart (Psalm xiv. 1).
Non aeris acervus et auri aegroto domini *deduxit* corpore febres.
Κάτθαν' ὁμῶς ὅ τ' ἀεργὸς ἀνήρ ὅ τε πολλὰ ἐοργώς.

§ 106. Tenses employed to define the verbal activity as already completed at some point of time in the past which the speaker has in mind, or to denote a past state resulting from a preceding activity. [PRAETERITUM PERFECTUM: § 76, I. 2 *b*.]

Here we have the meaning of the Present Perfect transferred to past time. The range of usage of the Past Perfect tense is similar in all the six languages, though the Greek Past Perfect brings the idea of a resultant past state into greater prominence than does the Past Perfect of the other languages; cf. § 103. When the Greek desired to make the preceding act prominent, he employed the Aorist, which in this use is to be translated by the English Past Perfect.

I *had seen* all that there was to be seen, so I came away.—We *had lived* and *loved* together.

Kaum *waren* wir *angekommen*, als die Nachricht eintraf.

Ex iis aedificiis quae *habuerant demigraverant.*

Il *avait travaillé* toute la journée (1st Past Perfect). —Nous sortîmes [sommes sortis], dès qu'il *eut fini* (2nd Past Perfect, sometimes called 'Passé Antérieur').

Ya *había acabado*, cuando entró (1st Past Perfect).— Luego que *hube acabado*, salimos (2nd Past Perfect).

Greek Past Perfects: Ἀτρέμας εὗδε, λελασμένος ὅσσ᾽ ἐπεπόνθει ('all that he had suffered,' Od. xiii. 92).—Ἡ Οἰνόη ἐτετείχιστο ('had been fortified' or 'was a fortified town', Thuc. ii. 18. 2).

Greek Aorists: Ἄλοχος δ᾽ οὔπω τι πέπυστο Ἕκτορος· οὐ γάρ οἵ τις...ἤγγειλε ('had reported', Il. xxii. 439).

§ 107. English and Spanish have a special continuous form to mark an *act* as having gone on up to a point of time in the past which the speaker has in mind: I *had been writing*; *Había* (or *Hube*) *estado escribiendo*.

§ 108. Tenses employed to mark the verbal activity simply as having taken place before the time of speaking. [PRAETERITUM INDEFINITUM: § 76, II. 1.]

The pure time-relation is here precisely the same as in the definite tenses belonging to § 103. In both cases the activity spoken of is prior to the time of speaking. But whereas the Present Perfects define the activity as *already completed at* the time of speaking, these indefinite tenses mark it as simply *prior to* the time of speaking. This distinction is, no doubt, a rather subtle one; for an activity that has taken place before the time of speaking is, at the time of speaking, completed; and *vice versa*. Yet there is an important psychological difference between these two aspects of the same time-relation—i.e. a difference which depends on how the activity is *regarded*. In the one case attention is directed to the abiding results of the prior action (§ 103), in the other merely to its priority. But to abstain from directing attention to the idea of completion is a very different thing from regarding the prior activity as *not* completed[1].

The meaning of simple priority to the time of speaking is expressed in English, German, Latin, and Greek by a tense which has also some other meaning—in English by the Past (§ 100), in German either by the Past (§ 100) or by the Perfect (§ 103), in Latin by the Perfect (§ 103), in Greek by the Aorist (§ 103). Thus all these English, German, Latin, and Greek tenses have a twofold meaning; but they coincide in being capable of expressing the meaning treated in this section. French and Spanish alone have a tense which is limited to this meaning, viz. the Past Historic[2] (derived from the Latin Perfect); but they too—especially French—employ the Perfect (§ 103) as a substitute.

[1] This point seems to have escaped the notice of some grammarians. For example, the Revised Latin Primer (1888–1924) offers a scheme of tenses (§ 105) in which *rogavi* 'I asked' is classified as expressing 'incomplete action' (side by side with *rogabam*), but *rogavi* 'I have asked' as expressing 'complete action'. This is really misleading. For if the pupil were to think this out, he would be driven to the conclusion that the Romans, that nation of strict and logical thinkers, as he is often told, could not discern the difference between a completed action (e.g. in *Veni, vidi, vici*) and an action that was not completed, but somehow regarded the former as the same as the latter, however much it differed in reality.

[2] Different names have been given to this French tense by French grammarians at different periods. In the seventeenth and eighteenth centuries it was often called the 'Passé Indéfini'—a term which was in

In recounting a number of past activities which took place in succession (one after the other), each is marked separately as having taken place prior to the time of speaking. When so used, the above mentioned tenses are commonly called 'narrative tenses', i.e. tenses answering the question *What happened next?* It should be observed that the question *how long* the activity lasted is quite irrelevant.

William the Conqueror *landed* in 1066. After the battle of Hastings he *ascended* the throne of England, and *reigned* for twenty-one years. He *was succeeded* by his son, William Rufus.

Schiller *wurde* im Jahre 1759 *geboren* (Past).—Wir *haben* uns gestern zufällig *getroffen*, und *sind* zusammen ins Theater *gegangen* (Perfects).—Um zwölfe Mittags *starb* er....Der Alte *folgte* der Leiche. Albert *vermocht*'s nicht....Handwerker *trugen* ihn. Kein Geistlicher *hat* ihn *begleitet* (Perfect—without difference of time-relation from the Pasts which precede. This is a very curious example of the use of the two tenses side by side, taken from Goethe's description of the death and funeral of Werther).

Hieme anni post urbem conditam DCCII Iulius Caesar commentarios suos de bello Gallico *scripsit*.—Verres inflammatus furore in forum *vēnit*; ardebant oculi, toto ex ore crudelitas eminebat (§ 100).

La bataille *recommença* avec fureur; la cavalerie chargeait (§ 100) pour la troisième fois, quand Blücher *arriva* (Past Historic).—Je *suis arrivé* à Londres hier soir; j'*ai soupé*, je me *suis promené*, je *suis allé* au

itself perfectly intelligible, but which was subsequently changed to its opposite—'Passé Défini'. Both these terms were officially banned by the French Ministry of Education in 1909; nowadays the term 'Passé Historique' is often employed.—The American Committee recommends the term 'Past Absolute' for this French and the corresponding Spanish tense.

spectacle, j'*ai joué* aux cartes (Perfects). This use of
the Perfect has been getting more and more common
during the last half century, and has to a great extent
ousted the use of the Past Historic, except in the strict
historical style.

El día 31 de Diciembre el ejército *entró* en Roma
(Past Historic).—Le *he visto* esta mañana (Perfect).
This use of the Perfect is very much less common
in Spanish than in French.

῏Ηλθον, εἶδον, ἐνίκησα (Plutarch; translated from
the Latin *Veni, vidi, vici*).—Ἐβασίλευσε δέκα ἔτη
(Herodotus ii. 157).—Ἡμέρη τε ἐγίγνετο (§ 100)
καὶ ἅμα τῷ ἡλίῳ ἀνιόντι σεισμὸς ἐγένετο (Id. viii.
64. But the contrast between the Past Imperfect and
the Aorist in narrative is on the whole much less
clearly marked in Greek than in Latin).

Obs. 1. From Alexandrian times onward the Greek Present
Perfect assumed the meaning of an Aorist: e.g. ἐξέθετο καὶ
πέφευγε (in an inscription of B.C. 88); ἦλθε καὶ εἴληφε
(Apocalypse v. 7).

Obs. 2. In Greek and Latin the Past Imperfect was sometimes
used as a narrative tense, i.e. to denote mere priority to the time
of speaking. See Brugmann-Thumb, Griech. Gram. § 552. 2;
Bennett, Syntax of Early Latin, Vol. I, pp. 32–35. This usage
was probably an inheritance from the parent language.

**§ 109. Tenses employed to mark the verbal activity simply as
about to take place after the time of speaking. [FUTURUM
INDEFINITUM: § 76, II. 2.]**

The tenses used in expressing this meaning in our six languages
have all the same range of meaning, and are therefore all called
by the same name, viz. Future. This term covers the two meanings of 'Future Imperfect' and 'Future Indefinite'; for the distinction between (i) an activity going on or habitual at some point
of time in the future which the speaker has in mind, and (ii) an

activity about to take place after the time of speaking, is not an important distinction in any language, though it *may* sometimes be drawn. The Stoic grammarians drew no such distinction in Greek; how far it can be drawn in that language is a question on which modern scholars are not agreed[1].

I *shall* [You *will*, He *will*] *see* what *will happen*.
Ich *werde* [Du *wirst*, Er *wird*] *sehen*, was sich *ereignen wird*.
Dies *veniet*.—Cras decima hora *cenabo*.
Le jour *viendra*.—Les enfants songent avec joie aux jouets qu'on leur *donnera*.—Quand il *reviendra*, je le lui *dirai*.
Mañana *será* otro día.—Pronto lo *sabrá*.—Eso es lo que *harán* mañana.
Ἀλλ' ἐγὼ διὰ παντὸς τοῦ βίου...τοιοῦτος φανοῦμαι (Plato, Apology 33 *a*).—Τὰ πολλὰ Πρωταγόρας ἔνδον διατρίβει, ὥστε καταληψόμεθα αὐτόν (Protagoras 311 *a*).

§ 110. English and Spanish have a special continuous form to mark an *act* as going on at some point of time in the future which the speaker has in mind: I *shall be writing*; *Estaré escribiendo*. But the other languages use the ordinary Future (§ 109) to express this meaning.

§ 111. On the use of the Present tense in expressions of futurity see § 79. This usage is especially common in the Germanic languages, which in the early days of their existence as a separate group had no other means of expressing futurity. In later times compound future tenses were developed; but the old use of the elastic Present survived: Duncan *comes* here tonight.—And when *goes* hence? (Macbeth i. 5. 60).—War must cease; otherwise we *perish* (Professor Gilbert Murray).—When [If] he *comes*, I shall

---

[1] See the thorough examination of this problem in Wackernagel's Vorlesungen über Syntax (Erste Reihe, 1920), pp. 192–208.

tell him the news.—*Kommt* Zeit, *kommt* Rat.—Wenn er *kommt*, werde ich es ihm sagen. So, too, in Latin—especially in Early Latin: see examples in Plautus (Mil. 1020, Trin. 156, etc.) and Cicero (ad Att. i. 4. 3, xiv. 11. 2, Verrines II, § 85) and Virgil (Aen. iii. 606, iv. 27). So, too, in French and Spanish: Attendez-moi, je *viens*.—S'il *vient*, je le lui dirai.—Mañana *llega* el rey.—Si eso *hace*, se le castigará. In Greek this usage is very common in verbs of 'going' and 'coming'; and it is not confined to these. In all our languages the usage must be regarded as an inheritance from the parent language.

§ 112. We have now come to the end of the Stoic scheme of tenses, which did not include the Future Perfect: see § 76. But this tense cannot be ignored even in Greek—still less in the other languages with which we are concerned. We have, then, to add this category:

Tenses employed to define the verbal activity as already completed at some point of time in the future which the speaker has in mind, or to denote a future state resulting from a preceding activity. [FUTURUM PERFECTUM.]

The tense used in expressing this meaning is the Future Perfect in all six languages.

Before this time tomorrow I *shall have gained* a peerage or Westminster Abbey (Life of Nelson). Der erfahrene Kenner...Beim ersten Blicke *wird gelesen haben*, Was ich ihm taugen kann, was nicht (Schiller, Don Carlos iii. 10. 26).—Unsere Hand wird den süddeutschen Brüdern entgegenkommend dargereicht werden, sobald der Norddeutsche Bund weit genug *vorgeschritten sein wird* (Speech from the throne)[1].

[1] The Future Perfect is not much used in ordinary German speech except to denote a probability, e.g. Wo *wird* er die Nacht *zugebracht haben*?—Es *wird* was andres wohl *bedeutet haben* (Schiller). In general German uses the Present or the Future or the Perfect instead of the Future Perfect.

Ille te nisi amabit ultro, id pro tuo capite quod dedit *perdiderit* tantum argenti (Plautus, Most. 2 1 1).—Tolle hanc opinionem, luctum *sustuleris* (Cicero, Tusc. i. 30)[1]. Après-demain nous *serons entrés* dans Orléans.—Quand j'*aurai repris* mes sens, je reprendrai le fil de mon histoire.—Il l'*aura oublié* (expressing probability). Mañana *habrá acabado.—Habrás oído* muchas veces (expressing probability).

Φράζε καὶ πεπράξεται (Aristoph., Plutus 1027; 'speak and it will be a *fait accompli*'.—*Ἢν δὲ μὴ γένηται, μάτην ἐμοὶ κεκλαύσεται, σὺ δ' ἐγχανὼν τεθνήξεις* (Clouds 1435; 'If this does not happen, I shall have had my whippings for nothing, and you will have died with a grin on your face'; i.e. when you are dead you will have had the laugh of me). In the active voice the future perfect meaning is generally expressed by compounding the Perfect (or sometimes the Aorist) Participle with ἔσομαι, e.g. ἐγνω-κότες ἐσόμεθα 'we shall have known'.

§ 113. English and Spanish have a special continuous form to mark the completion of an *act* which will have been going on at

---

[1] The Latin Future Perfect may also be used without the sense of completion, i.e. as an expression of simple futurity, for example in the main clause of the following sentence: Cum causam iustam deus ipse dederit, vir sapiens laetus ex his tenebris in lucem illam *excesserit* (Cicero, Tusc. i. 74). This usage is often found in Early Latin; but it has been pointed out by Kroll that in the large majority of instances it occurs at the end of iambic or trochaic lines, in which the form of the Future Perfect was metrically convenient (Berliner Phil. Wochenschrift, 1905, p. 102, and Neue Jahrbücher für das klass. Altertum, 1910, pp. 325 f.; cf. Sjögren, Zum Gebrauch des Futurums, 1906, p. 150). Kroll is of opinion that the Latin Futures and Future Perfects were originally synonymous and rival forms, created after the loss of the old Indo-European future, and that it was not till a later stage of the language that they were differentiated in use. In the hexameter too the choice of tense sometimes depends on metrical considerations: see Norden on Aen. vi. 89.

some point of time in the future which the speaker has in mind: *I shall have been writing*; *Habré estado escribiendo.*

§ 114. We have also to add to the Stoic scheme another category of tenses—that of *futures in the past*. The only kind of Future recognized by the Stoics was the tense in which the activity is future in relation to the time of speaking (§ 109). But futurity may also be regarded from a past point of view, i.e. as related to some point of time in the past which the speaker has in mind: an activity may be spoken of as *then* lying in the future. And this is a very common and necessary form of speech, e.g. 'I knew what *would happen*' (corresponding to 'I know what *will happen*'). Tenses expressing this meaning are found in the most ancient as well as in the modern languages of our family[1]. But in Greek and Latin this meaning was expressed by forms of speech which are not generally regarded as tenses—a future participle with a tense of past time, or some other equivalent expression; and modern German uses a tense of the subjunctive mood (*er würde schreiben*, or *er werde schreiben*).

§ 115. Tenses employed to mark the verbal activity as about to take place after some point of time in the past which the speaker has in mind. [FUTURUM IN PRAETERITO.]

The Future in the past is recognized by some recent French grammarians as a tense of the indicative; and is called by them *Le futur dans le passé*[2].

The Future in the past has two uses. In instances like the

---

[1] I call the attention of those who talk of the lapse of time as having "torn asunder languages that were once akin" to the fact that Sanskrit had a Future in the past, which was formed by turning a *sya*-Future into a tense of past time: an augment was added and the personal inflexions of past tenses were substituted for those of present tenses: e.g. from the Future *bhavi-sya-mi* 'I shall be' was formed *á-bhavi-sya-m*, which meant 'I should have been' or sometimes 'I should be'; in Vedic there is the form *á-bhari-sya-t* meaning 'he would take away'.

[2] For example by Professor Brunot in La Pensée et la Langue (1922), p. 515, and in L'Enseignement de la langue française (1909), p. 110. The American Committee recommends the abbreviated form 'Past Future'.

following there is nothing *conditional* about the tense; for no condition is expressed or implied:

> The King of Spain was a sickly child. It was likely that he *would die* without issue. A day *would* almost certainly *come* when the House of Bourbon might lay claim to that vast empire on which the sun never set (Macaulay).—The autumn days passed quickly over, and with them the last peaceful hours that Inglesant *would know* for a long time. Such a haven as this... *would* never *be* open to him again (Shorthouse).—A few days were to bring on the fatal fight of Edgehill, when the slain *would be counted* by thousands (Mark Lemon).

> > Thou sawest a glory growing on the night,
> > But not the shadows which that light *would cast*.
> > > (Tennyson, Epitaph on Caxton.)

> Je savais qu'il *arriverait* à dix heures.—Les enfants *seraient* heureux, croyait-il.—Les enfants songeaient avec joie aux jouets qu'on leur *donnerait*.—J'ai promis de le protéger contre quiconque l'*attaquerait*.

> Decía [Dijo, Ha dicho] que *llegaría* el día siguiente.

But in other instances this tense acquires the meaning of conditioned futurity, without ceasing to be a tense of the indicative mood. See § 118. iii[1].

§ 116. Tenses employed to define the verbal activity as about to be already completed after some point of time in the past which the speaker has in mind. [FUTURUM PERFECTUM IN PRAETERITO.]

The Future Perfect in the past stands in the same relation to the Future in the past as the Future Perfect (§ 112) stands to the Future (§ 109).

> I thought I *should have seen* some Hercules;...Alas this is a child (Shakespeare, Henry VI, Pt. I, ii. 3. 19).—Well did I hope This daughter *would have blest* my latter days (Rowe, Fair Penitent iv. 1).

> Le jeune homme répondit [a répondu] qu'il *aurait écrit* avant

---

[1] Darmesteter-Sudre, Grammaire Historique, Part IV, p. 156.

le lendemain.—Les enfants songeaient avec joie aux jouets qu'on leur *aurait donnés*.
Decía [Dijo, Ha dicho] que *habría acabado* el día siguiente.

§ 117. English and Spanish have a special continuous form of both these tenses (§§ 115, 116): *I should be writing*; *Estaría escribiendo*; *I should have been writing*; *Habría estado escribiendo*.

II. INDICATIVES WITH ACQUIRED MEANINGS (IN EXPRESSIONS OF UNREALITY; §§ 88, 89)

§ 118. Indicatives in expressions of unreality are found in Greek, French, and to some extent in Spanish:

(i) in expressions of unrealized or unrealizable wish introduced by εἴθε or εἰ γάρ in Greek and by *si* in French[1]:

(*a*) Εἴθ' ἔζη.—Εἰ γὰρ ἐδυνάμην.
Si nous *étions* à leur place!

(*b*) Εἴθ' ηὕρομέν σ', Ἄδμητε, μὴ λυπούμενον.
Si j'*avais su*!

(ii) in *if*-clauses of conditional sentences with an implication of unreality or reserve[1]. See examples below (under iii).

(iii) in expressions of conditioned futurity, i.e. futurity regarded as realizable only under certain conditions. This meaning is indicated in Greek by adding ἄν or κεν to a Past Imperfect or Aorist Indicative (§ 88), and in French and Spanish generally (but not always, cf. § 139) by a Future in the past or a Future Perfect in the past (§§ 115, 116), used with an acquired meaning: out of the idea of past futurity has been developed that of conditioned futurity[2]. In the following examples the expression

---

[1] In these constructions Spanish has the subjunctive, like Latin, German, and English.

[2] The Sanskrit forms mentioned in § 114 (note) have gone through exactly the same process of development as the corresponding French and Spanish forms. In Latin conditioned futurity is sometimes expressed by a Future participle with *eram, eras, erat* or *fui, fuisti, fuit*.

of conditioned futurity is combined with an *if*-clause implying unreality or reserve (ii above):

(*a*) Εἰ τοῦτο ἔλεγεν, ὀρθῶς ἂν ἔλεγεν.
S'il *disait* cela, il *aurait* raison.
Si esto dijese (Past Subjunctive), *tendría* razón.

(*b*) Εἰ τοῦτο εἶπεν, ὀρθῶς ἂν εἶπεν.
S'il *avait dit* cela, il *aurait eu* raison.
Si esto hubiese dicho (Past Perfect Subjunctive), *habría tenido* razón[1].

The condition need not be expressed by a separate clause; it is often only implied: Ἐβουλόμην ἂν εἰπεῖν.—Hésiter *serait* [*aurait été*] une faiblesse.—*Osaría* afirmar. Such sentences are often little different in meaning from cautious statements of present fact; e.g. Je *voudrais* bien voir çà!—No *podría* decírselo.

III. USES OF THE IMPERATIVE AND ITS TENSES

§ 119. The imperative mood has been used from the earliest Indo-European times in expressing the desire of the speaker that something may be done by (or may happen to) the subject of the imperative verb: its tone ranges from the abruptest command to a mere wish. These shades of meaning (command, request, entreaty, prayer, wish) may be distinguished in living speech by the intonation of the sentence.

Hang a calf-skin on those recreant limbs.—*Forget* me not.—O King, *live* for ever.—*Fare*well.
Schweige!—Du Heilige, *rufe* dein Kind zurück!—*Lebe*wohl.
Lictor, *obliga* manus, caput *obnubito*, arbori infelici *suspendito*.—*Da*, pater, augurium (Virgil, Aen. iii. 89).—*Vive vale*que (Horace, Sat. ii. 5. 110). The negative in Latin is *ne*, e.g. Ne *saevi*, magna sacerdos (Aen. vi. 544).

---

[1] This combination of a Past Perfect Subjunctive with a Future Perfect in the past is sometimes found in French, for example in the famous saying of Pascal: "Si le nez de Cléopâtre *eût été* plus court, toute la face de la terre *aurait été changée*".

Abandonnez la ville.—Ne *fermez* pas la porte.—*Ayez* pitié de moi.—*Soyez* heureux.—*Portez*-vous [*Amusez-vous*] bien.

Ven aquí, tú.—¡Santo Dios, paciencia *dad*me! In negatived expressions of desire Spanish uses the subjunctive (§ 126).

Παῦσαι (Soph. Antig. 280).—Μεῖνον παρ᾽ ἡμῖν καὶ συνέστιος γενοῦ (Eur. Alc. 1151).—Ἔρρωσο. The negative in Greek is μή, e.g. Μὴ θορυβεῖτε (Plato, Apology 21 *a*).

OBS. The imperative is often used to express a *supposition*: *Do* what you may (= Even if you do your utmost), you will not succeed.—*Ostendite* modo bellum, pacem habebitis (Livy vi. 18. 7).—*Bouge*, je te tue.—Προσειπάτω τινὰ φιλικῶς ὅ τε ἄρχων καὶ ὁ ἰδιώτης· τὴν ποτέρου πρόσρησιν μᾶλλον εὐφραίνειν τὸν ἀκούσαντα νομίζεις; (Xen. Hiero viii. 3, followed by ἐπαινεσάντων, θεραπευσάντων, and δόντων).

§ 120. In addition to the 2nd person, singular and plural, which all the six languages have in common (§ 119), Latin and Greek have a 3rd person, singular and plural:

obligato 'let him bind'; *obliganto* 'let them bind'.
λυέτω 'let him loosen'; λυόντων 'let them loosen'.

§ 121. French is peculiar in having a 1st person plural of the imperative—a meaning which is expressed in the other languages by the subjunctive (§ 126) or by an imperative-equivalent (§ 123):

Marchons! ('March we' or 'Let us march').

§ 122. Tenses of the Imperative.

(i) The Latin forms in -*to*, -*tote*, and -*nto* originally referred to a more remote future than the other forms of the imperative, and have therefore been called 'Future Imperatives'. But this distinction is clearer in Early Latin than in the classical period, when the longer and the shorter forms of the mood were to a great extent used promiscuously; see an example in § 119.

(ii) Some languages have a perfect imperative, but it is rarely used: e.g. *Have done.—Be gone.—Ayez abandonné* la ville, quand l'ennemi y entrera.—Πέπαυσο.—Ταῦτα ταύτῃ εἰρήσθω.

§ 123. Imperative-equivalents.

(i)   Formed with *shall, sollen* or *let, lassen*:

> Thou *shalt* not kill.
> Du *sollst* deinen Vater und deine Mutter *ehren.*
> *Let* him *do* it, if he dares.—*Let* us *sing.*
> *Lass* [*Lasst*] ihn kommen.—*Lass* [*Lasst*] uns singen.

The Latin *sine* is similarly used: *sine* modo ad*veniat* senex; *sine* modo *venire* salvom (Plautus, Most. 11 f.).

(ii) The Present Subjunctive (cf. § 126):

> *Kommen* Sie her (originally 3rd person, 'let them come here', but used as a polite expression of command in the 2nd person, 'come here').

(iii) The Future Indicative (cf. § 78):

> Post nonam *venies* (Horace, Epist. i. 7. 71; cf. *reddes* 17).
> Tu ne *tueras* point.
> No *matarás.*

(iv) The Infinitive:

> Still *stehen!*
> Ne pas se *pencher* au dehors.—Bien *faire* et *laisser* dire.
> *Venir* mañana.—Paciencia y *barajar* (Don Quixote).
> Πρὶν δ' ἂν τελευτήσῃ, ἐπισχεῖν μηδὲ καλέειν κω
> ὄλβιον, ἀλλὰ εὐτυχέα (Herod. i. 32).—Χαίρειν μετὰ
> χαιρόντων, κλαίειν μετὰ κλαιόντων (Romans xii. 15).

This use of the Infinitive is of early origin and wide-spread: it arises naturally from the datival character of the Infinitive. But it is hardly found in Latin till the post-classical period.

IV. USES OF SUBJUNCTIVES AND OPTATIVES
PROPER, WITH THEIR TENSES

§ 124. The whole trend of modern investigation into the history of the subjunctive and the optative has been to show that
each of these moods has two main types of usage. The subjunctive proper—i.e. the subjunctive as it was in the parent language
and continued to be in the usages of the mood that are common
to all the daughter languages—is divisible into (1) subjunctives
of will or volition, (2) subjunctives of futurity. And similarly
the optative proper is divisible into (1) optatives denoting wish,
(2) optatives that are commonly described as 'potential'; but
these 'potential optatives' turn out on scrutiny to be futuristic,
i.e. to express some kind of futurity[1].

There is, therefore, a remarkable parallelism between the
subjunctive proper and the optative proper: indeed the parallelism is even greater than appears at first sight, because the
distinction between *will* and *wish* is a very subtle one, which
in a large number of instances cannot be drawn without violence
or hairsplitting.

It seems, then, that a common classification of the subjunctive proper and the optative proper is possible:

(1) subjunctives and optatives of *desire*;

(2) subjunctives and optatives of *futurity*.

The second of these classes I subdivide into

(*a*) expressions of determined or unconditioned futurity.
Subjunctives and optatives that express this meaning I call
'prospective[2]'.

[1] Monro (Homeric Grammar, § 315) described this kind of optative as
"a softened Future, expressing expectation, or mere admission of possibility
(the English *may* or *should*)"; and he called it "quasi-Future".
[2] For the history of this category of the subjunctive see "The Prospective Subjunctive" by the present writer (Classical Review, Vol. VII,
1893) and "The Anticipatory Subjunctive in Greek and Latin" by Prof.
W. Gardner Hale (Chicago, 1894). The term 'prospective' is now so
widely adopted in Germany that it is sometimes claimed as a creation of
"die deutsche Wissenschaft". In the Report of the American Joint-Committee the term 'anticipatory' is recommended.

(*b*) expressions of conditioned futurity, i.e. futurity regarded as realizable only under certain conditions, expressed or implied.

And I further recognize as intermediate between expressions of desire and expressions of futurity, and possibly providing a link of connexion between them, a third category which I call expressions of *obligation* or *propriety*, i.e. what *ought* to be done.

My whole scheme of classification of the subjunctive and the optative will therefore be:

I. The Subjunctive proper and the Optative proper:
  (1) in expressions of desire (§§ 126–130);
  (2) in expressions of obligation or propriety (§§ 131–133);
  (3) in expressions of determined or unconditioned futurity (§§ 134–137);
  (4) in expressions of conditioned futurity (§§ 138–140).

II. Subjunctives and Optatives with acquired meanings (§§ 141–145).

In putting the four subdivisions of the first category in this order I do not commit myself to any theory as to the historical order of their development. We have really no means of judging which category of usage was the *earliest*; indeed it is possible that they all existed side by side from the first. And they may even be regarded as facets of one common meaning (§ 87, note). On the other hand each of them comprises a number of varieties, which have been regarded by some scholars as constituting separate classes.

The several tenses of the subjunctive and the optative are grouped under each of the above categories[1].

[1] The tense of the subjunctive commonly called 'Imperfect' in Latin, French, Spanish, and German is here called 'Past', in accordance with the recommendation of both the British and the American Terminology Committees. That the term 'Imperfect Subjunctive' is a misnomer for the Latin forms in *-rem, -res, -ret* has long been known to scientific grammarians: the formative element *-re-* has nothing to do with the *-ba-* which forms the Past Imperfect Indicatives in *-bam, -bas, -bat*; and the two sets of forms do not correspond in use, except in so far as they both belong to the sphere of past time. See, for example, Wackernagel, Vorlesungen (1920), I, p. 248, and Sommer, Handbuch der lat. Laut- und Formenlehre (1914), § 340.

§ 125. In the sequel I show that the old meanings of the subjunctive and the optative are still alive in modern languages and are expressed to a great extent by the mood called 'subjunctive' in English, German, French, and Spanish. But I do not claim as subjunctives all forms of speech in which these meanings are expressed. Modern English makes a large use of 'subjunctive-equivalents', e.g. expressions formed by combining a tense (indicative, subjunctive or imperative) of the verbs 'shall', 'will', 'may', 'let' with an infinitive. Thus instead of the subjunctive *write* we frequently say *shall write* or *may write* or *let...write*. Another very common substitute for the subjunctive is *am to*, *are to*, *is to* with an infinitive, e.g. 'He *is to write*', 'He *was to write*'. But it is obvious that to include all such equivalents as subjunctives would be to give a false impression of the relation of English to other languages. For the purpose of comparing English usage with the usage of other languages it is necessary to limit the term 'subjunctive' to such forms as correspond to the forms commonly called subjunctives in other languages—forms derived from subjunctives or optatives of the parent language or closely modelled thereon. In the following sections therefore (§§ 126–140) subjunctive-equivalents will be excluded from view, except in *translations* of subjunctives of other languages (inserted in brackets and enclosed in inverted commas), as in § 132, p. 96, § 135, p. 99, etc.

§ 126. Subjunctives and optatives in expressions of desire [§ 124, I (1)].

(i) *in simple sentences and main clauses.*

Here the Present subjunctive of English, German, Latin, French, and Spanish, the Perfect subjunctive of Latin, and the Present and Aorist subjunctive and optative of Greek, are used (like the imperative, but with various nuances of meaning) in expressing the desire of the speaker that something may be done by (or may happen to) the subject of the subjunctive or optative verb. This subject may be the speaker himself. These expressions of desire may be negatived (in Latin by *ne*, in Greek by μή, as with the imperative, § 119).

The following examples are so arranged as to correspond with the examples of the imperative in §§ 119–121. The 2nd person is put first, wherever a language has this use of the 2nd person; then comes the 3rd person, and finally the 1st person. But the 2nd person is comparatively rare, its place being generally taken by the imperative. In English a subjunctive in the 2nd person is indistinguishable from an imperative: e.g. 'You *be d—d*'.

God *forbid.*—God *save* the King.—Britannia *rule* the waves.—*Deny* it who can.—Devil *take* the hindmost. —Woe *betide* him.—*Make* we our sword-arm doubly strong, and *lift* on high our gaze (The Times, Jan. 19, 1915).—*Sit* we down (Hamlet i. 1. 33).

Er *lebe* hoch !—*Gehen* wir.—Ich *sei* in eurem Bunde der dritte (Schiller, Die Bürgschaft 139 f.).

Eas ('Go'; common in Early Latin: cf. *vivas*, Horace, Epist. i. 6. 66, *doceas, pandas* and *agnoscas*, Virgil, Aen. vi. 109, 407).—Ne *eas* ('Do not go', common in Early Latin; cf. Ne *pigrere*, Cicero, ad Att. xiv. 1. 2, Ne *sis*, Horace, Sat. ii. 3. 88).—Ne *transieris* Hiberum (Livy xxi. 44. 6; common in Livy and in the classical period)[1].—*Valeas* ('farewell' = *vale*, § 119).—*Cedant* arma togae (Cicero, De suis temporibus).—*Valeant* cives mei, *sint* beati; *stet* haec urbs, etc. (Pro Mil. 93).—*Sequamur*; *Placemus* ventos et Gnosia regna *petamus* (Aen. iii. 114 f.).—Ne *sim* salvus, si aliter scribo ac sentio (Cicero).

Dieu vous *bénisse* !—Dieu m'en *garde* !—A Dieu ne *plaise* !—*Vive* la République !—Qui m'aime, me *suive*. —*Sauve* qui peut !—*Périssent* les traîtres !—*Sois*-je du

---

[1] In this use of the Perfect subjunctive, which is comparatively uncommon in Early Latin, the tense has no sense of completion; compare the use of the Future Perfect indicative without the sense of completion (§ 112, p. 78 n.). In both cases the Perfect may be said to be aoristic. Compare the instances of the Aorist subjunctive in Greek, quoted below.

ciel écrasé, si je mens! (For the expression of this
meaning in the 1st pers. plur. see § 121.)
No *seas* tonto.—¡Bien venido *seas*!—No lo *crea* V.
—Bendita *sea* la madre que te parió.—*Plegue* a Dios.
—*Cantemos* todos a una.—Pues tenemos hogazas, no
busquemos tortas (Don Quixote).

Greek Subjunctives: Φέρε μάθῃς (Soph. Phil. 300,
rare).—Μή μ' ἀφῇς (ibid. 486; common in prohibi-
tions).—Μὴ τοῖς ὀλίγοις ἡ αἰτία προστέθῃ (Thuc.
iii. 39. 6).—Ἴωμεν.—Μὴ εἴπωμεν.—Φέρε ἴδω
(Herod. vii. 103).

Greek Optatives: Πίθοιό μοι (Homer, Od. iv. 193)[1].
—Ὦ παῖ, γένοιο πατρὸς εὐτυχέστερος (Soph. Ajax
550).—Μή τις ἀθεμίστιος εἴη (Homer, Od. xviii.
141 f.; cf. v. 8–10)[1].—Σὸν ἔργον εἴη τοῦτον ὀπτᾶν
(Aristoph. Lys. 839)[1].—Οἰκία δ' αὖτε κείνου μητέρι
δοῖμεν ἔχειν (Od. xvi. 385 f.; cf. the subjunctive in
384).—Πατρόκλῳ κόμην ὀπάσαιμι (Il. xxiii. 151;
cf. xv. 45 παραμυθησαίμην).—Μηκέτι ζῴην.

§ 127. Past and Past Perfect subjunctives in expressions of
unrealized or unrealizable wish:

O, *were* it mine! (Wordsworth, To the Queen 27).—*Were*
the people for us! (Browning, Strafford i. 2. 230).—O *had*
we some bright little isle of our own! (Moore).—*Did* I but
know!—*Had* I but *known*!
O *wären* wir weiter, o *wär'* ich zu Hause!—*Wäre* er doch
noch am Leben!—O *hätte* ich es nie *getan*!
Utinam hodie *viveret*!—Utinam illis temporibus *vixisset*!
Plût à Dieu que je pusse partir avec vous!—*Fût*-il déjà *venu*,
ce temps désiré! (For the indicative with *si* see § 118 (i).)

[1] Such optatives, expressive of command or request, are called 'prescriptive optatives'.

¡Ojalá *pluguiese* a Dios!—¡Ojalá me *hubieras dejado* morir!
—¡Ojalá *dejáras*me morir!

In Greek these meanings (originally expressed by the optative)
are expressed by an indicative (Past Imperfect or Aorist) used
with an acquired meaning: see § 118 (i).

§ 128. (ii) *in subordinate clauses.*

The desire expressed by the subordinate subjunctive or optative is not necessarily a desire of the speaker of the sentence;
contrast § 126.

(*a*) Clauses dependent on verbs of 'desiring', 'de-
manding', 'permitting', 'striving', or the like[1]:

I move that Mr A. *take* the chair.—The communists
demand that all men *be paid* according to their needs.
—The order of the day is that every man *die* at his
post.—Mind you *be* there in good time.—Let him
take heed lest he *fall* (= that he fall not).—I wish
I *knew* [*had known*].—O that I *were* a man!
Lasst nicht zu, dass das *geschehe*.—Sie bat ihn, dass
er sich *entferne*.—Der General befiehlt [befahl], dass
die Brücke *abgebrochen werde*.
Oro *venias*.—Peto abs te [Impero tibi] ut *maneas*.—
Permitte mihi ut *loquar*.—Ne *faciam*, inquis, omnino
versus? (Horace, Sat. ii. 1. 5 f.).—Hortatus est socios
ne *deficerent*.—Timeo ne *moriar*.—Timebam ne *mo-
rerer*.
Je prie Dieu qu'il vous *bénisse* (cf. § 126).—Je désire
que vous *restiez* ici.—Il va ordonner par son testament qu'on lui *fasse* les obsèques les plus simples.—

---

[1] In Latin, French, Spanish, and Greek verbs of 'fearing' take the construction of verbs of 'desiring' with a negative in the dependent clause,
which therefore is literally an expression of a desire that something may
not happen. Hence too the use of 'lest' instead of 'that' in some English
examples.

Je permets que vous le *fassiez.*—Je crains que je ne *meure.*—Il exigea que tout le monde *fût* là.—Il a voulu qu'on *parlât.*

Deseo que *venga.*—Temo no *venga.*—Deseaba que *viniese* [*viniera*].—Temió no le *perdiesen* el respeto.

Greek Subjunctives (in present or future time)[1]: Χρὴ φυλάσσειν καὶ προκαταλαμβάνειν ὅπως μηδ᾽ ἐς ἐπί-νοιαν τούτου ἴωσι (Thuc. iii. 46. 6).—Πράξουσιν ὅπως πόλεμος γένηται.—Βούλει λάβωμαι δῆτα; (Soph. Phil. 761).—Σκοπῶμεν μή τις ἀδικῆται.— Ὅρα μὴ πέσῃς (=Vide ne *cadas*).—Φοβοῦμαι μὴ ἐπιλαθώμεθα τῆς οἴκαδε ὁδοῦ.

Greek Optatives (in past time)[1]: Ἐμεμελήκει αὐτοῖς ὅπως ὁ ἱππαγρέτης εἰδείη (Xen. Hell. iii. 3. 9).— Σπεύδοντες ὡς Ζεὺς μήποτ᾽ ἄρξειεν θεῶν (Aesch. Prom. 203).—Ἐφοβεῖτο μὴ οὐ δύναιτο ἐκ τῆς χώρας ἐξελθεῖν.

But in dependent clauses of desire introduced by ὅπως Greek more commonly has the Future Indicative; and an Infinitive construction is used after certain verbs in both Greek and Latin.

§ 129. (*b*) Clauses of Purpose.

Lord God of Hosts, be with us yet, Lest we *forget*, lest we *forget* (Kipling).—The Spirit of Locarno must not be exaggerated or overstrained, lest it *fail* in its immediate purpose (The Times, Nov. 10, 1925).— Do this, lest a worse thing *befall* you.

Er spricht laut, damit er von allen *verstanden werde.* —Er sagte dies, damit kein Zweifel darüber *wäre.*

Venio ut *videam.*—Veni ut *viderem.*—Abit ne *videat.*

---

[1] 'In present time' means *standing in a sentence which as a whole refers to present time.* Similarly 'in past time' means *standing in a sentence which as a whole refers to past time.* On subjunctives in past time see p. 92, n. 2.

—Abiit ne *videret*.—Mittit [Misit] legatos qui *deliberent* [*deliberarent*][1].

Viens que je te *dise* un secret.—Je vous le disais afin que vous le *fissiez*.—Ils racontaient cela pour que nous *eussions* confiance.

Acércate para que te *vea*.—Se escondió a fin de que no le *pudiesen* encontrar.

Greek Subjunctives (in present time; denoting a present purpose)[2]: Φίλων δεῖται ἵνα [ὅπως] συνεργοὺς ἔχῃ.—Μὴ φθόνει τοῖς εὐτυχοῦσι, μὴ δοκῇς εἶναι κακός (poetical for ἵνα μὴ δοκῇς).

Greek Optatives (in past time; denoting a past purpose): Φίλων ἐδεῖτο ἵνα [ὅπως] συνεργοὺς ἔχοι.

But relative clauses denoting purpose (present or past) take the Future Indicative in Greek: Πέμπει ['Έπεμψε] πρέσβεις οἵτινες συμβουλεύσουσιν, lit. 'who shall take counsel'; cf. the use of the Future Indic. as an imperative-equivalent (§ 123 (iii)).

§ 130. (*c*) Clauses of condition (expressing a supposition).

Here the subjunctive or optative is postulative, i.e. it is used in expressing a desire that something be supposed or granted for the sake of argument. Such subjunctives or optatives are clearly akin to subjunctives and optatives of command or wish (§ 126; compare the same use of the imperative, § 119, Obs.): *Go* not my horse the better, I must become a borrower of the

---

[1] This use of the subjunctive in relative clauses of Latin is regarded by some grammarians as prospective (§ 136); compare the use of the Future Indicative in Greek relative clauses (below) and the use of the subj. in the following German and French instances: Hier sitz' ich, forme Menschen nach meinem Bilde, ein Geschlecht *das mir gleich sei* (Goethe, Prometheus); Je cherche pour gérer mon affaire une dame *qui ait longtemps habité le quartier*.

[2] The Subj. is also found in past time, i.e. the mood is often not adjusted to the past point of view: Τὰ πλοῖα κατέκαυσεν, ἵνα μὴ Κῦρος διαβῇ. See Goodwin, Moods and Tenses, §§ 318, 339.

night (Shakespeare, Macbeth iii. 1. 26).—*Be* England what she will, With all her faults she is my country still (Charles Churchill, The Farewell 27).—One here will constant be, *come* wind, *come* weather (Bunyan).—Der Mensch erfährt, er *sei* auch wer er mag, Ein letztes Glück und einen letzten Tag (Goethe).—*Vendat* aedes vir bonus; *norit* ipse vitia earum, ceteri *ignorent*: vitia emptori dicere debet (Cicero, de Off. iii. 13, § 54). —*Vienne* un second hiver aussi rude, nos rosiers seront gelés (lit. '*come* a second winter').—*Vengan* sobre lo que vinieren, ellas vienen las más galanas señoras (Don Quixote).—*Sea* lo que fuere.

The nature of the subjunctive in such clauses is not a whit changed when the clause is introduced by a word meaning 'if' or 'though'. A clause like 'If my horse go not the better' is simply a development of '*on condition* my horse go not the better': for *if* is a locatival dative of an old Germanic word meaning 'condition' (*ibu* = on condition); but it has been developed into a subordinating word, called a conjunction (*if* = on condition that). *Though* is a pronominal adverb formed from the old Germanic stem *tha-*: originally demonstrative (like the German *doch*), it has become a subordinating conjunction (= in view of this, that). The history of the Latin, French, and Spanish *si* and the Greek εἰ is similar. They are all developments from demonstrative adverbs meaning 'so', from one of which was also formed the Latin *sic* 'thus', by adding the suffix *-ce*. The word 'so' is sometimes used in English and old-fashioned German as a subordinating conjunction: 'No matter how it be in tune, *so it make* noise enough' (= provided that it make; Shakespeare, As you like it, iv. 2. 10; cf. ii. 3. 30); '*So* ihr bleiben werdet an meiner Rede, so seid ihr meine rechten Jünger' (Luther's translation of St John viii. 31)[1].

---

[1] Similarly 'so that'=provided that; e.g. "Every fact, *so that* it be a fact, is of importance in science" (Sir Oliver Lodge in The Observer, Feb. 13, 1927). We also get in Latin combinations like *sic si* or *ita si* ('so if'), *sic ut* or *ita ut* ('so as'), *ita ut ne* ('so as not'), used with restrictive conditional meaning; e.g. *Ita probanda est clementia ut adhibeatur severitas* ('provided that sternness be brought to bear', Cicero, de Off. i. 25, § 88). Exactly the same construction was used in a recent letter to The Times

Examples of *if*-clauses with the subjunctive or optative: If this *be* so, we are all at fault.—Let us not insist on it, even though it *be* true.—Omnes, si in Italia *consistat*, erimus una (Cicero, ad Att. vii. 10; cf. Horace, Od. ii. 2. 4; 14. 6; 17. 14; iii. 3. 7).—Si Júpiter no *lloviere*, aquí estoy yo que lloveré. —Δυστάλαινα τἄρ' ἐγώ, εἰ σοῦ στερηθῶ (Soph. O. C. 1442). —'Ω παρθέν', εἰ σώσαιμί σ', εἴσει μοι χάριν; (Eur. Andromeda, frag. 126).

Exactly the same usages are found with tenses of past time: If it *were* so, it was a grievous fault (Shakespeare, Jul. Caes. iii. 2. 84; 'if it were' = supposing it to have been).—Here was a leader who cared not who ruled Judaea, so that (= provided that) justice *were observed* (Morning Post, Dec. 24th, 1926).— Captain Fryatt was only carrying out the orders of his superiors and was therefore guiltless, even if the order itself *were* a violation of international law (The Times, May 12th, 1919).—Si vivere *vellet*, Seianus rogandus erat (Seneca, ad Marciam de consolatione, 22. 6; 'if he wanted to live, he had to ask it as a favour of Sejanus').—Deciens centena *dedisses* huic parco, quinque diebus nil erat in loculis (Horace, Sat. i. 3. 15 f.).

In the above instances there is no implication of unreality in the *if*-clause: *if it be* means simply 'supposing it to be'; *if it were* simply 'supposing it to have been', 'supposing that it was'. There is therefore only a shade of difference between these subjunctives and indicatives[1], and where there is no difference of form between the two moods in English, they are indistinguishable: e.g. *If he wanted it*, why did he not ask for it?

But in conditional sentences whose main clause has an expression of conditioned futurity the conditioning clause

(April 16, 1926) by the Archbishop of Canterbury: "The largest liberty should, I think, be left to the parish clergy in the matter, *so only that* they *fail* not to give opportunity for earnest and united prayer".

[1] There is a similar use of the subjunctive in clauses introduced by such words as 'whoever', 'whenever', in English and Greek, and by *quamvis* in Latin: e.g. Πᾶς ποιητὴς γίγνεται οὗ ἂν Ἔρως ἅψηται 'whomsoever Love *touch*' (here we should ordinarily say 'touches'); Οὗ ἅψαιτο Μίδας ἐγίγνετο χρυσός 'Whatsoever Midas *touched* turned into gold'; Senectus quamvis non *sit* gravis ('though it be not burdensome', lit. 'be it as little burdensome as you will'—*quam vis*), tamen aufert viriditatem.

generally acquires an implication of unreality: O *wert* thou in
the cauld blast, I'*d shelter* thee (Burns; here 'wert thou' implies
'thou art not').—*Had* we never *loved* sae blindly, we *had* ne'er
been broken-hearted (Burns; here 'had we never loved' implies
'we have loved' or 'we did love').—Typical instances of such
conditional sentences in English, German, and Latin, which
agree in this use of the subjunctive, will be found in § 139. For
the corresponding sentences in French, Spanish, and Greek see
§ 118 (iii).

**§ 131. Subjunctives and optatives in expressions of obligation
or propriety [§ 124, I (2)].**

These subjunctives and optatives are used in expressing what
is to be done (= *ought to be done*) or *was to be done* (= *ought to have
been done*) by the subject of the subjunctive or optative verb,
i.e. what is (or was) *incumbent* on that subject, whether he or
anyone else desires (or desired) it or not. Contrast §§ 126–130.

§ 132. (i) *in simple sentences and main clauses.*

The non-dependent subjunctive and optative of obligation
or propriety are found only in Latin and Greek; in the other
four languages this meaning is expressed by equivalent forms of
speech.
The negative is in Latin *non* or *ne* (*ni*), in Greek μή.

(*a*) Questions:

Quid ego nunc *faciam*? (Plautus, Men. 963; 'What am I to
do now?').—Quid ego *agam*? (Most. 378; cf. 662 and Capt.
531)[1].—Quid ego ni *fleam*? (Mil. 1311; cf. *non*, Capt. 139).
Greek Subjunctives: Ὤμοι ἐγώ, πᾷ βῶ, πᾷ στῶ, πᾷ
κέλσω; (Eur. Hec. 1056).—Ποῖ τις οὖν φύγῃ; (Soph. Aj.
403)[1].—Πότερον βίαν φῶμεν, ἢ μὴ φῶμεν εἶναι; (Xen.
Mem. i. 2. 45). Optative (rare): Theocritus xxvii. 24.

---

[1] These examples occur in monologue, and are commonly called
'Deliberative Questions'. But the same use of the mood occurs in other
contexts, in which the term 'deliberative' is quite inapplicable or at any
rate inadequate. The term 'dubitative' is just as bad or worse; see Class.
Review, Vol. XVI, p. 166.

Nonne ego illi argentum *redderem*? (Trin. 133; 'Was I not
to pay him the money?').—Nonne *reprehenderes* luxuriosos,
Epicure? (Cic. de Fin. ii. 22; 'Ought you not to have
blamed the sensualists?').—Quid *faceret*? (Plautus, Rud. 379,
'What was he to do?').—Non *redderet*? (Virgil, Ecl. iii. 21)[1].

(*b*) Statements:

Maneam, opinor (Trin. 1136; 'I had better wait, I think').
—*Invenias* argentum (Terence, Phorm. 540; 'You are to
find the money', answering the question Quid *faciam*?).—
Non *redderes* (Trin. 133; 'You ought not to have paid').—
Adservaret (Rud. 379; 'He ought to have kept watch').

Such statements are found in all periods of Latin (negatived
by *non*):

A legibus non *recedamus* (Cic. pro Clu. 155; 'We ought not
to swerve from the laws').—*Cedat*, opinor, forum castris (Pro
Mur. 30; 'The forum ought, I suppose, to yield to the camp').
—*Feras*, non *culpes*, quod mutari non potest (Publilius Syrus,
1st century B.C.; 'One should put up with, and not find fault
with, what cannot be changed').—*Sciamus* quis sit de quo
referas (Pliny, Epist. ix. 13. 7; 'We ought to know').—At
tu dictis, Albane, *maneres* (Virg. Aen. viii. 643; 'You ought
to have kept your word').—Eadem me ad fata *vocasses* (Aen.
iv. 678: Past Perfect synonymous with Past subjunctive).

§ 133. (ii) *in subordinate clauses*.

(*a*) Dependent Questions[2].

Quid *faciam* nescio ('What I am to do I don't know').—
Quid *facerem* nesciebam ('What I was to do I didn't know').
—Deliberaverunt utrum flumen *transirent* necne.—Satis erat
causae quare Caesar in Dumnorigem *adverteret* (Caesar, B. G.
i. 19; 'why Caesar was bound to punish Dumnorix').

---

[1] There is no use of the Greek optative that corresponds to this use of
the Latin past subjunctive in non-dependent questions (denoting *what was
to be done* in past time); but cf. § 133 *a*, p. 97.

[2] Contrast these dependent questions as to obligation or propriety with
dependent questions as to a matter of fact (§ 142 (*b*)).

Greek Subjunctives (in present time): Ἀπορῶ ποῖ τράπωμαι.
—Βουλευόμεθα εἴτε διαβῶμεν τὸν ποταμὸν εἴτε μή.
Greek Optatives (in past time): Ἠπόρουν ποῖ τραποίμην.
—Ἐβουλεύσαντο εἴτε διαβαῖεν τὸν ποταμὸν εἴτε μή.

(b) Dependent Statements.

In sentences containing dependent statements of this kind (English, German, Latin, French, and Spanish) the meaning of obligation or propriety expressed by the subjunctive of the subordinate clause is generally anticipated in the main clause:

It is of the most imperative importance that everything possible *be done* to make sure of large harvests (President Wilson, April 1917).—It is better that he *die* than that justice *depart* out of the world (Carlyle).—'Tis time that I *were gone* (Tennyson, Morte d'Arthur 163).

Es ist nicht immer nöthig dass das Wahre sich *verkörpere* (Goethe).—Es ist nur billig [gerecht], dass er seine Schulden *bezahle*.

Adeam optumumst (Plautus, Asin. 448).—*Dicamus* senibus legem censeo (Merc. 1015).—Aequom videtur tibi ut ego, alienum quod est, meum esse *dicam*? (Rud. 1230 f.).—Concedetur profecto verum esse ut bonos boni *diligant* (Cicero, de Amic. 50).—Tres video sententias ferri: unam ut eodem modo erga amicum affecti *simus* quo erga nosmet ipsos, alteram ut...*respondeat*, tertiam ut...tanti *fiat* ab amicis (ibid. 56).—Tua ratio est ut secundum binos ludos mihi respondere *incipias* (in Verrem, Actio i. 34).—Tempus est [Locus est] ut multa *dicantur* (Cic.).—Restat ut *doceam* (de Nat. Deor. ii. 154).—Socrates respondit sese meruisse ut amplissimis honoribus *decoraretur* (de Orat. i. 232).

Il a mérité que vous l'*aimiez*.—Mon avis est que vous *preniez* garde.—Il faut [convient] que vous le *sachiez*.—Il vaut mieux qu'on y *aille*.—Il fallait que je le *fisse*.—Cela valait qu'on y *allât*.

Ha merecido que le *quieran* sus amigos.—Conviene [Hace falta] que lo *sepa* V.—Es menester que el que ve la mota en ojo ajeno *vea* la viga en el suyo.

In Greek (and also often in Latin after impersonal expressions such as *aequum est*) the accusative with the infinitive is used in dependent statements of obligation.

(*c*) Other subordinate clauses.

> Quid in me admisi, ut loqui non *audeam*? (Plautus, Men. 712; 'What crime have I committed, that I *should* not *venture* to speak?').—Circumscribit nos terminis quos non *excedamus* (Livy xxi. 44. 5; 'which we are not to pass over').—Quid attinet fingere aliquos qui, cum luxuriose viverent, non *reprehenderentur* eo nomine dumtaxat, cetera *caverent*? (Cicero, de Fin. ii. 21; 'who were not to be blamed on that account at any rate, but were only to beware of the other things').—Non tantum maerorem senatui mors Clodii afferebat ut nova quaestio *constitueretur* ('had to be appointed', Cic. pro Milone 13).—Dignus est [erat] quocum in tenebris *mices* [*micares*]. C'est un homme qui est digne qu'on le *plaigne*.—Je ne vois rien qui vous *retienne*.
> No veo nada que lo *impida*.

§ 134. Prospective subjunctives and optatives [§ 124, I (3)].

Prospective subjunctives and optatives are used in expressions of futurity dissociated from the idea of desire (§§ 126–130) and from that of obligation (§§ 131–133). The futurity that they denote is an unconditioned or determined futurity and is thus distinguished from the conditioned futurity which will be discussed below (§§ 138 f.).

The meaning of a prospective subjunctive or optative differs only by a shade from that of a future indicative : it corresponds pretty closely to that of the English 'shall' when used to denote a futurity that is *bound to be realized*. This use of 'shall' is seen in such expressions as 'Dost thou think, because thou art virtuous, there *shall be* no more cakes and ale?—Yes, by Saint Anne, and ginger *shall be* hot i' the mouth too' (Shakespeare, Twelfth Night, ii. 3. 123 ff.). In dependence on a tense of past time 'shall' of course becomes 'should'—the activity being thus marked as in prospect from a past point of view.

§ 135. (i) *in simple sentences and main clauses.*

Here the prospective subjunctive and optative (as distinct from an equivalent expression) are found only in Latin and Greek (Homeric and Hellenistic):

Saepe tribus lectis *videas* cenare quaternos (Horace, Sat. i. 4. 86—'you shall see', cf. ii. 2. 114; Virgil, Georg. i. 386, Aen. iv. 401; Plautus, Most. 243, Poen. 585, 831, Amph. 1060. Similarly 'you shall hear [know, think]', Mil. 689, 761, Pseud. 1176, Most. 278, Cas. 562).—Iniuriam facilius *facias* quam *feras* (Publilius Syrus 280, cf. 185).—Ubi mortuus sis (§ 136), ita *sis* ut nomen cluet (Plautus, Trin. 496, 'When you shall be dead, dead you shall be'; cf. 671)[1].

Greek Subjunctives (negatived by οὐ): Οὐ γάρ πω τοίους ἴδον ἀνέρας, οὐδὲ ἴδωμαι (Homer, Il. i. 262).—Οὐκ ἔσθ' οὗτος ἀνήρ, οὐδ' ἔσσεται οὐδὲ γένηται (Od. xvi. 437).— Καί ποτέ τις εἴπῃσιν (Il. vi. 459).—Ὤμοι ἐγώ, τί πάθω; τί νύ μοι μήκιστα γένηται; (Od. v. 465). With ἄν or κεν: οὐκ ἄν τοι χραίσμῃσι βιός (Il. xi. 387, cf. 433).—Ἐγὼ δέ κ' ἄγω Βρισηΐδα (Il. i. 184).—Εἰ ἐν τῷ ὑγρῷ ξύλῳ ταῦτα ποιοῦσιν, ἐν τῷ ξηρῷ τί γένηται; (Luke xxiii. 31; cf. xi. 5, 6).

Greek Optatives (negatived by οὐ)[2]: Ῥεῖα θεός γ' ἐθέλων καὶ τηλόθεν ἄνδρα σαώσαι (Od. iii. 231).—Οὐ μὲν γάρ τι κακώτερον ἄλλο πάθοιμι (Il. xix. 321). With ἄν or κεν: Ἄλλον κ' ἐχθαίρῃσι βροτῶν, ἄλλον κε φιλοίη (Od. iv. 692). Obsolescent in Hellenistic Greek.

§ 136. (ii) *in subordinate clauses.*

Here the prospective subjunctive or optative is found in all our six languages.

Here will I stand till Caesar *pass* along (Shakespeare, Jul. Caes. ii. 3. 11).—Friedrich Wilhelm took a newspaper till the job *were done* (Carlyle).—She made up

---

[1] In Horace, Sat. i. 1. 62 the same kind of subjunctive is found in subordination to *quia*.

[2] The Prospective Optative in simple sentences and main clauses is not at present recognized by grammarians.

her mind to look before she *leaped* (= should leap).
—Mr Bonar Law stated that the Dominion Govern-
ments were to have a voice in the peace negotiations,
when the time *came* (= should come).

Unsere Truppen brachen die Brücke ab, ehe die Feinde
kämen ('should come').—Wir warteten, bis er *käme*
('should come').

Expectare dum [donec] hostium copiae *augeantur*
summae dementiae est (Caesar, B. G. iv. 13).—Nullo
pacto potest prius haec in aedis recipi quam illam *ami-
serim* (Plautus, Mil. 1095 f.).—Priusquam se hostes
ex terrore *reciperent*, exercitum in Suessiones duxit
(B. G. ii. 12).—Sabellis docta ligonibus versare gle-
bas…sol ubi montium *mutaret* umbras (Horace, Odes
iii. 6. 38–41). Compare 'Dic quod te *rogem*' (Plautus,
Asin. 29) with 'Quod *rogabo* dicite' (Men. 1105).

Attendez jusqu'à ce que je *vienne*.—Le blessé sera
mort avant que le médecin *soit arrivé*.—Ne sortez
pas que je ne vous *aie parlé*.—On le garda au fond
d'une forteresse, jusqu'à ce qu'on *eût tiré* de lui une
grande rançon.

Mientras *quede* esperanza de salvarle, trabajaremos.
—Cuando *venga*, se lo diré.—Esperamos hasta que
viniese.

Greek Subjunctives (in present or future time),
negatived by μή in Attic: Ἔσσεται ἦμαρ ὅτ' ἄν ποτ'
ὀλώλῃ Ἴλιος ἱρή (Il. vi. 448).—Οὐκ ἔσθ' ὅς κέ σ'
ἕλῃσι (Il. xxiii. 345).—Οὐκ ἔσθ' ὅς τις θάνατον φύγῃ
(xxi. 103). Attic instances: Περιμένετε ἕως ἄν αὐτὸς
κελεύσῃ (Plato, Phaedo 59 *e*).—Οὐ πρότερον κακῶν
παύσονται αἱ πόλεις πρὶν ἂν οἱ φιλόσοφοι ἄρξωσιν
(Repub. vi. 487 *e*).—Ὅταν δὴ μὴ σθένω, πεπαύ-
σομαι (Soph. Antig. 91; cf. 773 and Ajax 657 ἔνθ'

ἄν, 1074 ἔνθα μή without ἄν, 1086 ἂν λυπώμεθα[1].
—Ἐὰν τοῦτο λέγῃ [εἴπῃ], ἁμαρτήσεται[2]. Hellenistic
instances: Ἐλεύσονται ἡμέραι ὅταν ἀπαρθῇ ὁ νυμ-
φίος (Mark ii. 20; cf. xiii. 30 Οὐ μὴ παρέλθῃ ἡ
γενεὰ αὕτη μέχρις οὗ πάντα ταῦτα γένηται).—
Διακόνει μοι ἕως φάγω καὶ πίω (Luke xvii. 8; cf.
ii. 26 πρὶν ἢ ἂν ἴδῃ τὸν Χριστόν).

Greek Optatives (in past time), negatived by μή in
Attic: Οὐδ᾽ ἔτλη εἰρύσθαι μέγα δῶμα διαμπερές,
ἧος ἵκοιτο (Homer, Od. xxiii. 151).—Οὐκ ἔθελεν
φεύγειν πρὶν πειρήσαιτ᾽ Ἀχιλῆος (Il. xxi. 580).
Attic instances: Περιεμένομεν ἕως ἀνοιχθείη τὸ
δεσμωτήριον (Plato, Phaedo 59 e).—Ὁπότε καιρὸς
εἴη, ἔμελλε στρατεύειν.—Κρύψασ᾽ ἑαυτὴν ἔνθα μή
τις εἰσίδοι, βρυχᾶτο (Soph. Trach. 903; cf. Homer,
Od. v. 240). Obsolescent in Hellenistic Greek.

§ 137. Clauses of Result, denoting a consequence or effect that
is only *contemplated* or *in prospect*, as distinct from clauses of
actual result (§ 145 a), naturally admit this construction.

Such clauses took the subjunctive in Anglo-Saxon; and instances are found in the English Bible, e.g. Exodus xxi. 12,
'He that smiteth a man so that he *die* shall be surely put to
death'. But in English of the present day this subjunctive is
generally replaced by a subjunctive-equivalent ('so that he *shall
die*') or by the indicative ('so that he *dies*') or by an infinitive
('If a man is smitten so as *to die*'; 'He is not the man *to die*
without making an effort to save himself').

In German of the present day the use of the subjunctive in
such clauses is hardly known: the indicative is almost exclusively
used.

---

[1] See Prof. A. C. Pearson in Proceedings of Cambridge Philological
Society, 1922, p. 28, and Classical Quarterly XI, 1917, pp. 68 f.
[2] This is the ordinary form of a conditional sentence with an open condition referring to future time.

In Latin, French, and Spanish the prospective subjunctive is
the ordinary construction in such clauses; but Greek has either
an indicative or an infinitive:

Ita paravi copias...facile ut *vincam*, facile ut *spoliem* meos
perduelles (Plautus, Pseud. 579 ff.; 'that I am bound to be
easily the victor and to despoil my antagonists': cf. Asin.
313).—Ita te hinc ornatum amittam, tu ipsus te ut non
noveris (Rud. 730; 'that you shall not know the look of
your own face').—Non videor mihi sarcire posse aedis meas
quin (= ut non) totae perpetuo *ruant* (Most. 146 f.).—Haec
omnia sic agentur, ut bellum intestinum *sedetur* (Cicero, in
Cat. ii. 28; cf. i. 32; Orator 137, 138, containing forty-
three such subjunctives).—Humanior est quam ut ignoscere
non *possit*.—Hannibali nimis laeta res est visa maiorque quam
ut eam statim animo capere *posset* (Livy xxii. 51. 3, literally
'too full of joy and greater than that he should be able to
comprehend it'. Compare Shakespeare, Cor. i. 4. 16 f.,
'We'll break our walls rather than they *shall pound* us up').
—Longius aberant quam quo telum adici *posset* (Caesar, B. G.
ii. 21).—Fortem posce animum....Qui spatium vitae ex-
tremum inter munera *ponat* Naturae....*Nesciat* irasci, *cupiat*
nihil, etc. (Juvenal, Sat. x. 358 ff.).
Soyez si braves que vous ne *craigniez* rien.—Apprenons autre
chose qui *soit* plus joli.
De tal manera pelearemos que los enemigos *huyan*.—Cuén-
tanos otra cosa que *sea* mas alegre.

**§ 138. Subjunctives and optatives in expressions of con-
ditioned futurity** (i.e. futurity regarded as realizable only under
certain conditions, expressed or implied; § 124, I (4)).

Conditioned futurity is futurity under the shadow of a mental
reserve. In proportion as the shadow is light, the expression of
conditioned futurity (*would be*) approaches to an expression of
simple futurity (*is likely to be* or *will be*): in proportion as the
shadow is dark, the expression of conditioned futurity approaches
to an expression of unrealizability (*is not likely to be*).

§ 139. The idea of conditioned futurity may be expressed by a past tense of the indicative, used with an acquired meaning, as we have seen (§ 118 (iii)); but in English, German, and Latin it is expressed by a tense of the subjunctive or an equivalent thereof. And in French and Spanish a Past Perfect Subjunctive may be equivalent to a Future Perfect in the past. A *Past Subjunctive* is in its very nature akin to a *Future* in the *past*; for the idea of futurity is inherent in the subjunctive proper and the optative proper[1].

The following are the main types of sentence formed by combining a conditioning clause (§ 130, p. 95) with a clause of conditioned futurity in English, German, and Latin:

(*a*) If he *said* [*Did* he *say*] this, he would be (= *were*) right.
Wenn er dies *sagte, würde* er Recht *haben* [*hätte* er Recht].
Si hoc *diceret* [*dicat, dixerit*], recte *diceret* [*dicat, dixerit*][2].

(*b*) If he *had said* [*Had* he *said*] this, he would have been (= *had been*) right.
Wenn er dies *gesagt hätte* [*Hätte* er dies *gesagt*], *würde* er Recht *gehabt haben* [*hätte* er Recht *gehabt*].
Si hoc *dixisset*, recte *dixisset*.

In Greek conditioned futurity was originally expressed by an optative with ἄν or κεν, and this usage survived with a restricted sphere of meaning in classical times[3]. But some of its meanings were taken over by the indicative with ἄν: see §88 and § 118 (iii).

§ 140. Subjunctives and optatives of conditioned futurity may be used in subordinate clauses of various kinds, as in the English

[1] Thus in Latin a future participle with *eram* or *fui* may be equivalent to a Past Perfect Subjunctive of conditioned futurity, e.g. *Emendaturus*, si licuisset, *eram* (=Emendavissem; Ovid, Tristia i. 7. 40).
[2] The Present subjunctive is often used in Early Latin as synonymous with the Past subjunctive; e.g. Tu si hic *sis*, aliter *sentias* (Terence, Andr. 310); cf. Plautus, Bacch. 636, Curc. 164, Epid. 331, Mil. 1371. But in Ciceronian and Augustan Latin the Present subjunctive generally refers to future time. The Past subjunctive is often synonymous with the Past Perfect subjunctive in Early Latin, e.g. Deos credo voluisse; nam ni *vellent*, non *fieret* (Plautus, Aul. 742; cf. Mil. 30, Rud. 590).
[3] i.e. with reference to future time, e.g. Εἰ τοῦτο λέγοι [εἴποι], ὀρθῶς ἂν λέγοι [εἴποι]=Si hoc dicat, recte dicat.

'I do not doubt that it *would be* [*were*] well to do this'.—'If it *would be* [*were*] well to do this, why not do it at once?'—'He is a man who *would do* the right thing, if he saw it clearly'.

V. SUBJUNCTIVES AND OPTATIVES WITH ACQUIRED MEANINGS (RELATING TO A MATTER OF FACT: § 124, II)

§ 141. We now turn to a different class of instances—those in which the subjunctive and the optative have acquired functions which they did not possess in the parent language. The common feature of these later usages is that the moods have been so far changed in meaning that they have come to relate to a matter of fact, yet without being synonymous with indicatives. For these developed usages are rarely expressions of bare fact; they have generally a nuance of meaning which the indicative mood is incapable of expressing; and one of them, so far from expressing fact, provides a means of disclaiming responsibility for a statement: here the speaker indicates by the use of the subjunctive or optative mood that what he has to report is something for which he himself *does not vouch.*

Owing to this process of development the moods of the daughter languages are only partially coincident in meaning with those of the parent language. And the acquired meanings of these moods play an exceedingly important rôle in the syntax of the daughter languages—so much so that they are apt to strike the beginner in Latin or French as the most characteristic of all the usages of the subjunctive, just because he meets with them so frequently. On the other hand the subjunctive and the optative of the daughter languages share in a great many of the meanings of the original subjunctive and optative, so that within their spheres of meaning the nucleus of a 'subjunctive proper' and an 'optative proper' may be clearly distinguished (§§ 126–140).

The precise history of the new usages of the moods in the developed daughter languages is often difficult to trace, and need not be discussed in detail here. In some instances the peculiar use of the subjunctive in Latin, French, Spanish, and the Germanic languages is probably of composite origin; i.e. it is due to the interaction of more than one cause. For the purpose in hand it is sufficient simply to register the existence of these acquired usages, without attempting an historical explanation of them.

In this field we must not expect to find so much agreement between the daughter languages as was found above (§§ 126–137). For each language has gone its own separate way. Yet even here there are some important coincidences between the acquired usages of the several daughter languages—coincidences which seem to be due in the main to the similar working of the human mind in similar circumstances.

§ 142. The use of the optative and the subjunctive in expressions of 'oblique speech' (*Oratio Obliqua*) is one of the developments which took place later than the period of the parent language: it grew up independently but on parallel lines in Greek, in Latin, and in the Germanic languages. Here the Greek optative and the subjunctive of the other languages indicate that the speaker or writer is merely reporting a statement or opinion of another person or of himself on another occasion.

(*a*) The Greek optative is thus used, depending on a tense of past time, in dependent statements and dependent questions as to a matter of fact: Εἶπεν ὅτι φιλαθήναιος εἴη ('that he was a lover of Athens').—Ἠρόμην εἰ φιλαθήναιος εἴη ('whether he was a lover of Athens').

(*b*) The Latin subjunctive is similarly used in dependent questions as to a matter of fact, and it is not limited to dependence on a tense of past time. Thus we get not only instances like *Quaerebant quis esset et unde venisset* but also (perhaps owing to the working of analogy) instances like *Quaero quis sit et unde venerit*. In the latter of these constructions there is no 'obliquity'; nor has the subjunctive the meaning of obligation or propriety which it has in dependent questions of the kind quoted in § 133 *a*. What the precise origin of this Latin usage is cannot be determined with certainty; but one thing is clear: it is due to an encroachment of the subjunctive on the sphere of the indicative.

For in Early Latin we find the indicative frequently used in dependent questions as to a matter of fact (e.g. *Scio quid dictura es*, Plautus, Aul. 174), and this construction is occasionally found even in the classical period, and to a greater extent in late Latin. The use of the subjunctive, in fact, did not become a rule of Latin syntax till the time of Cicero, and even then it was not an absolute rule, as we see in Cicero's letters. Where it is used it is used with a meaning somehow acquired. See § 90.

(*c*) In dependent *statements* as to a matter of fact Latin of all periods ordinarily used the accusative with infinitive construction; but *quod* with a finite verb came to be used in popular speech as equivalent to the accusative with the infinitive. The earliest example of *quod* with the subjunctive is found in a passage of Plautus (Asin. 52): *Equidem scio iam filius quod amet meus istanc meretricem*[1]. The next earliest instance is *Legati renuntiaverunt quod Pompeium in potestate haberent* (Bell. Hisp. 36. 1)[2]. Instances in dependence on verbs of emotion ('rejoicing', 'grieving', 'wondering', etc.) are common in all periods of Latin, e.g. *Milites indignabantur quod conspectum suum hostes ferre possent* ('should be able').—*Mirabile est quod non rideat haruspex cum haruspicem viderit* (Cic. de Nat. Deor. i. 71; cf. de Divin. ii. 51).

(*d*) The Germanic subjunctive of oblique speech is still fully alive in modern German:

Sie glaubten dass niemand etwas davon *wisse*.—Wir fürchteten dass er nicht *kommen werde* (or *würde*).—Niemand wusste ob es wahr *sei*.

---

[1] On this much disputed passage see Löfstedt, Peregrinatio Aetheriae, p. 118.

[2] This use of *quod* with the subjunctive, or sometimes with the indicative, became very common after the middle of the second century A.D., as a substitute for the accusative with the infinitive—in Apuleius, Gellius, the Scriptores Historiae Augustae, Eutropius, the Vulgate, and the Fathers of the Church: see G. Mayen, *De particulis* quod, quia, quoniam, quomodo, ut, *pro acc. cum infin. post verba sentiendi et declarandi positis* (Kiel, 1889) and Löfstedt (*op. cit.* pp. 116–121). See also the recent Grammar of the Vulgate by Plater and White (Oxford, 1926, pp. 120 f.), where it is shown that in the Old Testament the subjunctive is more often used than the indicative in this construction.

§ 143. Similar subjunctives relating to a matter of fact are found in Dependent Statements and Dependent Questions in English (though not in common parlance), in French, and in Spanish:

It would be grossly unjust if the impression were left that General Pétain's success *were* due to German default in military engineering science (Birmingham Daily Post, Oct. 25, 1917).—I wonder whether it *be* true.—I wondered whether it *were* true.—If she be not so to me, What care I how fair she *be*? (George Wither).—Even those who had often seen him were at first in doubt whether this *were* truly the brilliant and graceful Monmouth (Macaulay).—The imperishable story of the battles of the Salient is vividly described below in a special article by Field-Marshal Sir William Robertson, in the course of which he replies to those who asked if (= whether) the sacrifice *were* worth while (Morning Post, July 23, 1927).

In Modern French and Spanish these subjunctives are found in dependence on verbs of emotion and also in subordination to any negative, interrogative, or conditioning clause:

Je me réjouis [Je regrette, Je m'étonne] qu'il *soit* parti.
Je ne dis pas [Croyez-vous, Si vous vous apercevez] qu'il *soit* malade.
Me alegro [Me extraño, No me pesa] que se *haya* ido.
No digo [¿Cree V......, Si nota V......] que *esté* enfermo.

But in earlier French the construction was not thus limited[1].

§ 144. Some instances of the subjunctive in subordinate clauses are most simply explained as due to the influence of a subjunctive in the superordinate clause: that is to say, the subordinate clause takes on the character of the clause to which it is subordinate, and adopts its mood. Thus a clause which *in itself* would require an indicative may take a subjunctive in subordination to another subjunctive, e.g. 'If only I knew what he *wanted*', which implies 'I do not know what he *wants*'. Such instances of 'attraction' or 'assimilation' of mood are psycho-

---

[1] See Darmsteter-Sudre, Grammaire Historique, Part IV, p. 122.

logically easy to explain, and they are found in many languages. In all such instances the meaning of a subjunctive proper is not perceptible, and the mood may be said to be used with an acquired meaning or with no meaning at all. But the question thus opened up is a large one and cannot be discussed in detail here[1].

§ 145. Latin has subjunctives relating to a matter of fact in two other important constructions: in these Greek and modern languages generally employ the indicative:

(*a*) Clauses of Actual Result[2]:

> Tam paratus fuit ad dimicandum animus hostium ut ad galeas induendas tempus *defuerit* 'that time *was lacking*' (B.G. ii. 21). —Erat ita non timidus ad mortem ut in acie *sit* ob rempublicam *interfectus* (Cic. de Fin. ii. 20, § 63).—Siciliam ita perdidit ut ea restitui in antiquum statum nullo modo *possit* (Id., Verrines, Actio i. 12).

The origin of these subjunctives is probably to be found in the uses mentioned in § 133 (*c*) and § 137, i.e. they were developed out of subjunctives proper denoting what was in some sense *bound to happen*. A suggestion of some such meaning is often discernible in instances where the Present or the Past tense of the subjunctive is used. For instance in *Tanta vis probitatis est ut eam etiam in hoste diligamus* the meaning 'so great that we are *bound to love* it even in an enemy' is at least not excluded. Hence it is that these subjunctives are so often best translated by infinitives: e.g. *Numquam tam male est Siculis quin aliquid facete dicant* (Verrines II. iv. 95), 'The Sicilians are never in such trouble *as not to say* something witty'. It is chiefly in instances with the Perfect (like those quoted above) that the meaning of bare fact is the only obvious one.

---

[1] For instances in Latin see Tenney Frank, Attraction of Mood in Early Latin (1904), and Bennett, Syntax of Early Latin, I, pp. 305–315.

[2] Here the indicative is sometimes found in Latin itself subsequently to the middle of the second century A.D. See Löfstedt (*op. cit.* p. 254).

(*b*) *Cum*-clauses denoting Time, Cause, or Contrast:

Cum *esset* Caesar in Gallia Citeriore, certior fiebat Belgas coniurare (B. G. ii. 1).

Cum id *nuntiatum esset*, in Galliam Ulteriorem contendit (ibid. i. 7).

Cum non amplius octingentos equites *haberent*, impetum fecerunt (ibid. iv. 12).

This construction was a development of the classical period of Latin literature[1]. In Plautine Latin *cum* (or, as it was then written, *quom*) regularly took the indicative (§ 90), as in Aulularia 178 *quom exibam domo* 'when I was leaving home', Rudens 378 *quom scibatis* 'seeing that you knew', and 383 *quom servat* 'although he watches'. When a subjunctive is found after *quom*, it generally has prospective or postulative meaning, as in Asinaria 185 *se ut quom videat gaudeat* 'in order that when he shall see him (*or* supposing him to see him) he may be glad'. There are a few passages which do not fall under this rule (e.g. Rud. 1124) and one or two in which the reading is uncertain (e.g. Truc. 381); but on the whole it may safely be said that many Plautine indicatives must have sounded strange to Cicero[2]. Yet there is no logical justification for the usage of the classical period: for there is nothing in the idea of cause, and nothing in the adversative meaning expressed by 'although', that involves the use of the subjunctive mood[3]. The subjunctive of the Ciceronian *cum*-clauses is, therefore, not a subjunctive proper, but a subjunctive with a meaning somehow acquired.

On the *ever*-clauses of Livy and Tacitus see § 90. A subjunctive in an *ever*-clause is notionally justified when the clause has conditioning force ('whenever' = if at any time, supposing that at any time). But in the usage of Livy and Tacitus the subjunctive was not limited to clauses of this character.

---

[1] Occasional instances occur earlier, but the construction did not *establish itself* till the classical period.

[2] In quoting Plautus Cicero sometimes unconsciously substitutes a subjunctive for an indicative, e.g. *exirem* for *exibam* in Aul. 178 : see De Divin. i. 65.

[3] *Quod, quia,* and *quamquam* ordinarily take the indicative.

RETROSPECT

On a general survey of the facts marshalled in the preceding chapters one conclusion seems to stand out prominently, viz. that the usages of the six languages here selected for examination admit of being classified on a common basis, and that there is a surprising identity of usage in these languages. There are also differences between the individual languages; but the lines of cleavage do not always run between ancient languages on the one hand and modern languages on the other.

The common basis of classification here adopted is that to which the science of comparative grammar points, viz. Indo-European syntax. Indo-European syntax is not to be identified with the syntax of any one of the ancient members of the Indo-European family of languages: it is the syntax which is common to them all—Sanskrit, Greek, Latin (and its descendants), the Germanic and the Slavonic languages, and others.

But there is one feature of modern languages to which many grammarians have pointed as marking a deep-seated difference of structure in the languages of modern Europe when compared with the ancient languages of Greece and of Rome, viz. the replacement of certain cases (the genitive and the dative) by phrases formed with prepositions, and the replacement of certain simple tenses by compound tenses, formed by combining a participle or an infinitive with a finite verb. The importance of these differences has been greatly exaggerated; but they *are* differences, and they must be frankly faced, and if possible accounted for. Modern English and the Romance languages generally have gone farther than Greek and Latin in developing case-phrases at the expense of cases, and compound tenses at the expense of simple tenses. But I have already shown in Chapter 1 (§ 70) that case-phrases are not an innovation of modern languages and that their development at the expense of cases is a process which began in ancient times; and the same thing may be said of compound tenses and simple tenses, as I will proceed to prove.

Compound tenses are not new creations of modern languages. Classical Greek had a multitude of such expressions; so too had Latin, especially in its later stages. In fact all the compound tenses found in modern languages have their prototypes in ancient languages. The perfect passives used in 'the letter *is written*', 'der Brief *ist geschrieben*', 'la lettre *est écrite*' have the same structure and meaning as the compound tense used in the Latin 'epistula *scripta est*'; and the Spanish 'la carta *está escrita*' corresponds word for word to a Latin 'charta *stat scripta*'. The perfect actives *ai écrit* and *he escrito* are direct descendants of the Latin *habeo scriptum*—a form of speech which seems to have originated in popular Latin usage, but is not uncommon even in the literary language of Cicero and Caesar: e.g. *cognitum habeo* (= cognovi, j'ai connu), *compertum habeo* (= comperi), *satis dictum habeo* (= satis dixi), ea quae Stoici *habent collecta* (= collegerunt), perfidiam Aeduorum *perspectam habebat* (= perspexerat). The English *have [had] written* and the German *habe [hatte] geschrieben* are formed on exactly the same principle, and may indeed have originated under Latin-French influence. The English continuous tenses (*am writing, was writing*, etc.) were no doubt modelled on the combination of the verb 'be' with an adjective; for example, the Anglo-Saxon *hīe wǣron blissiende* 'they were rejoicing' was modelled on *hīe wǣron blīþe* 'they were blithe'[1]. But so too were the corresponding Greek and Latin expressions: e.g. φεύγων ἐστί 'is fleeing' (= φεύγει, Aesch. Choeph. 136), δρῶν ἦν 'was doing' (= ἔδρα, Soph. Ajax 1324)[2]; *currens erat* 'was running' (= currebat, Bell. Hisp. 29. 2). This combination of a present participle with a tense of *sum* is, no doubt, rare in classical Latin; but it became common in certain late Latin writers, e.g. *negans sum* (= nego), *credens eram* (= credebam), *sequentes fuerunt* (= sequebantur or secuti sunt)[3]. The Spanish continuous tenses (*estoy*

[1] Sweet, New English Grammar, § 2204.
[2] In Hellenistic Greek such combinations were widely used; see Blass-Debrunner, Grammatik des neutestamentlichen Griechisch (5th ed., 1921), § 353.
[3] Löfstedt, Peregrinatio Aetheriae, pp. 245–9; cf. Diez, Roman. Gram. iv, p. 200. Compare in Early Latin *ut sis sciens* (= ut scias, Plautus and

escribiendo, estaba escribiendo, etc.) are similar formations, the gerund being substituted for the present participle, as in Latin instances like *bellum ambulando* (= ambulantes) *confecerunt* (in Cic. ad Fam. viii. 15. 1), or *quis talia fando temperet a lacrimis?* (Virg. Aen. ii. 6). The Romance futures *écrirai* and *escribiré* are direct descendants of the Latin *scribere habeo* 'I have to write' (Cic. ad Att. ii. 22. 6), which came to be used with the sense of necessity and futurity in the popular Latin of imperial times and the language of the Early Christian Church, for example by Tertullian (ovis ad victimam *duci habens* 'a sheep that is to be led to slaughter'; adversus Marcionem iv. 40) and by Jerome (quae nunc fiunt, hi qui *nasci habent* scire non poterunt 'those who are to be born', i.e. those who are not yet born; in Eccl. i). The English compound futures[1], formed with a verb of volition or obligation (he *will write*, I *shall write*), seem at first sight far removed from Greek and Latin expressions of futurity; but here too we have noteworthy parallels in both Greek and Latin. The verb ἐθέλω 'I will' not infrequently forms with an infinitive a future-equivalent, as in Τί λέξαι δέλτος ἥδε μοι θέλει; 'what will this tablet tell me?' (Eur. Hipp. 865), and in many passages of Herodotus (e.g. εἰ ἐθέλοι ἡ χώρη ἐς ὕψος αὐξάνεσθαι ii. 14); and in late Latin *volo* with an infinitive is often nothing more than a future-equivalent, e.g. *servire volunt* (= servi erunt; Corippus, Johanneis 6. 89); cum vidisset speciosum corpus super rogum *velle poni*, intuens magistrum ait... (Historia Apollonii 26). A parallel to the English future with *shall* is found in

Terence). Similar expressions are found in Plautus, Capt. 925 (*carens fui*), Curc. 87, Most. 141, Poen. 660, Rud. 943, Truc. 125.

[1] Jespersen denies that *will* ever forms a compound future with the pure sense of futurity; he says (Phil. of Gram., p. 282) that it always retains its original sense of volition, and must therefore be parsed apart from its object-infinitive. He seems to be quite in earnest about this theory; see p. 260 (2) and p. 50 of the work quoted, in which we are told that his objection to calling '(he) will come' a future tense is not that 'will' is a separate word: "Nothing would hinder us from saying that a language had a future tense, if it had an auxiliary that really served to indicate future time". But *will he succeed* in ruling out pure futurity from among the meanings of *will* with an infinitive? *Will* not his theory *turn out* to be a will o' the wisp?

the late Latin use of *debeo* with the infinitive, as in *facere debeo* (= faciam), and in some instances of *facere habeo* (lit. 'I have to make' = I shall make). The English expressions 'I am about to write' and 'I am going to write' are formed on exactly the same principle as the Greek μέλλω with the infinitive and the Latin *eo* with the supine (*spectatum it*, lit. 'he is going to see' = he will see). The German *werde schreiben* did not come into general use as a future till the period of 'Neuhochdeutsch' (sixteenth century); but even here a classical parallel may be found. *Ich werde schreiben*, lit. 'I become to write', suggests the idea of a starting point of action—the idea of beginning; and the verb *incipio* with the infinitive is used in late Latin as an expression of futurity, e.g. *incipit ire* = iturus est, *incipiens navigare* = navigaturus: cf. *incipissit facere*, almost = faciet, Plautus, Capt. 802.

The development of compound tenses side by side with simple tenses, and to some extent at their expense, is thus seen to be a process that has been going on since very early times; like the corresponding development of case-phrases (§ 70), it is by no means a *differentia specifica* of modern languages, though it bulks larger in the later than in the earlier forms of all the languages of our family.

Compound tenses, like case-phrases, seem to have arisen mainly from a desire for explicitness of expression. They are the result of a process of building up new forms of speech by combining two independent elements in a single composite expression, which may or may not be equivalent in meaning to some previously existing simple expression. In some instances the component elements which lay side by side in these composite forms of speech coalesced, so as to form a single word. The Latin past imperfects in *-bam* are a case in point. They originated in composite expressions, formed by combining a verb-noun (or, as the late Professor Skutsch thought, a verb-adjective, i.e. the present participle) with a past tense of the old verb of 'being' or 'becoming' (root *bhū*), e.g. *fere bam* (or *fam*), literally 'I-was a-bearing' or 'I-was bearing'; and these two elements subsequently coalesced into the single word *ferebam*. It is to be noted that Latin and the other Italic dialects never

had any simple form of the past imperfect indicative corresponding to the Greek ἔ-φερο-ν and the old Indian á-bhara-m. In the
French écrirai and the Spanish escribiré the two elements of
which these forms originally consisted (écrire ai and escribir he,
both representing the Latin scribere habeo, and originally written
as two words) have coalesced into a single word. It is obvious
that no hard and fast line can be drawn between a composite
group consisting of two words on the one hand and a single
word on the other. Yet it is upon the flimsy foundation of this
distinction that a false antithesis of 'analytical languages' and
'synthetical languages' has been set up[1].

The process of building up new forms of expression has been
going on at all times in the history of the Indo-European
languages. It is probably going on at the present day. Its pace
was no doubt accelerated when phonetic change rendered many
of the old inflected forms obscure or unrecognizable. Thus at
the period when the Romance languages were developed out of
local varieties of popular Latin it became desirable to find less
ambiguous expressions for some of the Latin cases and tenses.
But these new forms were created out of old materials and on
the analogy of previously existing composite expressions. The
same thing happened when Anglo-Saxon passed into Middle
English.

If this is anything like a true account of what happened, it
follows that there has been no breach of continuity in the
history of Indo-European speech, and that the attempt of
Jespersen and other grammarians to rebuild the edifice of grammar on lines which dissociate the structure of modern languages
from that of ancient languages involves a wholesale distortion
of historical fact and a misrepresentation of modern usage.

That the organic unity of a whole family of languages cannot
be adequately set forth on the narrow basis of six languages
of that family I am well aware. Nevertheless my inadequate
sketch may serve to reaffirm and reinforce an inference to which

---

[1] For an excellent criticism of the term 'synthetical' see Jespersen,
Progress in Language (1894), p. 347, and Language (1922), p. 421 f. But
the term 'analytical' is quite as misleading, as involving the idea of
decomposition.

the study of comparative syntax points, viz. that most of the grammatical constructions which live on the lips of the speakers of modern languages and are enshrined in the great literatures of the modern world are identical with constructions that were current in the ancient worlds of Greece and Rome, and may indeed be traced back to a far earlier period, when the parent language was spoken in its original habitat, wherever that may have been, in (say) the third millennium B.C. These 'syntactic types', if I may use the expression, have persisted from ancient to modern times; but they too have had their developments. Hence the emergence of syntactic varieties, diverse among themselves, yet linked together by that mysterious formative principle which controls their development and maintains their identity amid all their vicissitudes of external form. There is, then, such a thing as a common Indo-European syntax—common to all the languages of the family, modern as well as ancient— and its importance, both theoretical and practical, is great. For upon the recognition of a fundamental community of syntax depends the scientific justification of the principle of uniformity of grammatical terminology and classification, the practical value of which as an instrument of teaching is not disputed.

ADDENDA

The following notes, suggested by the friends who have read my proof sheets (*Preface*, p. ix), are additions for which there was no room on the pages as set up in type.

§ 3. Dr Mackail would have liked to see something about the history of "that curious and anomalous word *declension*. Why not *declination*, as in French and Italian ?"

§ 6. To my friend Colonel Mantell of Bath, who takes a great interest in psychology and languages, and with whom I have discussed many of the crucial points in the book, I owe the psychological justification for regarding some objects as in a sense 'causative', and the French limerick.

§ 9. My former pupil Mr C. T. Onions, Co-editor of the O.E.D., raises a question of terminology. If the term 'case' is defined as I define it, what is a 'case-form'? A form of a form? My answer is that by a 'case-form' I mean a form which *enters into* a case as one of its elements (e.g. § 4, p. 4). I conceive of a case as a dual entity having two elements in it—a form and a relation. The form might be called its body and the relation its soul. A 'case-form' is, then, the body of a case, and a 'case-relation' (§ 8, p. 7, etc.) its soul. My definition of the term 'case' (§ 9) combines these two elements of form and relation.

§ 11 (ii), p. 12. Mr Frank Richards of Bath remarks that the distinction of cases is often a matter of common sense. For example a writer of Latin wishing to say that certain savages were not cannibals might have written *Homines non edunt*—which would be sufficiently intelligible.

§ 70. Prof. Macdonell says that the converse loss of prepositions began in the Indian classical languages long before the vernaculars arose. In his Sanskrit Grammar for Students (3rd ed., 1927), §§ 176–9, he points out that only three prepositions out of twelve were left in Sanskrit as compared with Vedic—the others being replaced by cases used adverbially.

§ 108, p. 74. Prof. Macdonell (Vedic Grammar, pp. 343 f.) quotes a curious parallel to the combination of tenses in my quotation from Goethe.

§§ 121, 122. Prof. Macdonell points out that Sanskrit has a 1st person plural of the imperative. A pandit once said to him, "How much more perfect Sanskrit is than other languages! It has a 1st person imperative." I refer to this form in § 87, p. 63, as the only survival in Sanskrit of the Indo-European subjunctive. The fact that a subjunctive has become an imperative is an important point in my general theory of the subjunctive, as the late Prof. J. H. Moulton once pointed out to me. In my statement (§ 121) "peculiar" means "peculiar among the six languages here considered." Prof. Macdonell adds (with reference to § 122) that Vedic uses the form in -*tāt* for the 2nd person imperative pretty often ; see his Vedic Grammar for Students, § 131, p. 125.

Retrospect, p. 112. The Rev. W. E. Plater of Halstock has carefully examined the context of my quotation from Tertullian, and thinks that the idea of *predestination* (the fulfilment of prophecy) is prominent in *duci habens*.

INDEX

The references are to the sections excepting where the pages of the Preface and Retrospect are referred to (by p).—The letter n *means* foot-note.

modus 74
Monro, Dr D. B., 124 n.
mood 72–74 ; definition of, 77, 84 ;
developed usages of moods 91,
92, 118, 119–145

names of moods and tenses 82
narrative tenses 108
nominative 13, 18, 20 ; nominative
absolute 59, 61 n., 63
nubo 36 *b*, n.

'objective' case 8
objective genitive 52 (iv)
obligation, expressions of, 131–133
oblique cases 1
of in genitive-phrases 49 ; from
Latin *de* 70
optative 73, 87, 88 n.; classification
of uses, with references to sections, 124 ; expressing conditioned
futurity 139
oratio obliqua 142
order of words 4, 11 (i), 77
overlapping of cases 7 ; of moods
and tenses 78, 81

parco 36 *b*, n.
parent language, cases in, 13
partitive genitive 52 (x)
passé défini and *indéfini* 108 n.
passive constructions 24, 26, 35, 37
past historic 108
past imperfect indicative 100–102
past perfect indicative 76, 106
Pearson, Prof. A. C., 136 n.
perfect indicative 103 ; subjunctive
in negative commands 126 n.
phonetic change 12, 17
phrasing 11 (iii)
populus, vocative, 22 n.
possessive genitives 52 (i)
prepositions 65, 67 ; cases with, 68,
69

prescriptive optative 126 n.
present indicative 79, 80, 95–99, 111
present perfect 103–105
'preterite' 85 n.
price, genitive of, 52 (vii)
priority to the time of speaking 108
prospective subjunctive and optative
124, 134–137
πτῶσις 1, 4–6, 73
purpose, clauses of, 129

Quintilian 14
quod with the subjunctive 142 *b*

range of meaning, of cases 4 ; of
moods and tenses 78
respect, genitive of, 52 (iii)
result, clauses of, 137, 145 *a*

Sanskrit 87, 114 n., 118 n., p. 110
Sanskrit grammarians, *Preface* p. vi f.
Slotty, Dr F., 87 n.
so, as subordinating conjunction, 130
sociative-instrumental 13, 14, 16 ;
sociative-instrumental datives 46 ;
sociative-instrumental ablatives
56
Sommer, Dr F., 124 n.
Stoic grammarians 1, 75, 76, 94
studeo 36 *b*, n.
stylistic innovations 90, 142 *b*
subjunctive 73 ; in English 85 ; history of, 87 ; classification of uses,
with references to sections, 124
subjunctive-equivalents 86, 125
syncretism 14
'synthetical' languages, *Retrospect* p.
114

tense 75, 76 ; definition of, 77 ; tenses
of the indicative proper 94–117 ;
of the indicative with acquired
meanings 118 ; of the subjunctive
and optative 124 ff.

For EU product safety concerns, contact us at Calle de José Abascal, 56–1°,
28003 Madrid, Spain or eugpsr@cambridge.org.

www.ingramcontent.com/pod-product-compliance
Ingram Content Group UK Ltd.
Pitfield, Milton Keynes, MK11 3LW, UK
UKHW012333130625
459647UK00009B/253